S-ANON

Twelve Steps

S-ANON
International

Family Groups

S-Anon Twelve Steps
© S-Anon International Family Groups, Inc., 2000

P.O. Box 17294
Nashville, TN 37217

Library of Congress Catalog Card No. 99-75782
ISBN #978-0-9676637-0-8

S-ANON
International

Family Groups

S-Anon Conference Approved Literature
First printing   2000
Second printing   2005
Third printing   2010

Printed in the United States of America.

For information write or call the S-Anon International Family Groups office:
S-Anon International Family Groups, Inc.
P.O. Box 17294
Nashville, TN 37217
Phone: 615-833-3152 Toll-Free: 800-210-8141
E-mail: sanon@sanon.org
http://www.sanon.org

∽

God, grant me the serenity

To accept the things I cannot change,

Courage to change the things I can,

And wisdom to know the difference.

∽

ACKNOWLEDGMENTS

⚬

The materials excerpted from *Alcoholics Anonymous* and *Twelve Steps and Traditions* are reprinted with permission of Alcoholics Anonymous World Services, Inc. (A.A.W.S.) Permission to reprint these excerpts does not mean that A.A.W.S. has reviewed or approved the contents of this publication, or that A.A. necessarily agrees with the views expressed herein. A.A. is a program of recovery from alcoholism only — use of these excerpts in connection with programs and activities which are patterned after A.A., but which address other problems, or in any other non-A.A. context, does not imply otherwise.

Grateful acknowledgment is made for permission to reprint the following:

Excerpts from *Alcoholics Anonymous*. Copyright 1939, 1955, 1976, 2001 by Alcoholics Anonymous World Services, Inc.: New York, NY. Reprinted by permission of Alcoholics Anonymous World Services, Inc.

Excerpts from *Twelve Steps and Twelve Traditions*. Copyright 1952, 1953 by Alcoholics Anonymous World Services, Inc.: New York, NY. Reprinted by permission of Alcoholics Anonymous World Services, Inc.

Excerpts from *Al-Anon's Twelve Steps and Twelve Traditions*. Copyright 1981 by Al-Anon Family Group Headquarters, Inc.: Virginia Beach, VA. Reprinted by permission of Al-Anon Family Group Headquarters, Inc.

Excerpt from *Dilemma of the Alcoholic Marriage*. Copyright 1972 by Al-Anon Family Group Headquarters, Inc.: Virginia Beach, VA. Reprinted by permission of Al-Anon Family Group Headquarters, Inc.

Excerpts from *How Al-Anon Works for Families and Friends of Alcoholics*. Copyright 1995 by Al-Anon Family Group Headquarters, Inc.: Virginia Beach, VA. Reprinted by permission of Al-Anon Family Group Headquarters, Inc.

Excerpts from *Paths to Recovery: Al-Anon's Steps, Traditions and Concepts*. Copyright 1997 by Al-Anon Family Group Headquarters, Inc.: Virginia Beach, VA. Reprinted by permission of Al-Anon Family Group Headquarters, Inc.

CONTENTS

❧

S-ANON PREAMBLE
TO THE
TWELVE STEPS

S-Anon is a fellowship of people who share their experience, strength and hope with each other so that they may solve their common problems and help others to recover. The only requirement for membership is that there be a problem of sexaholism in a relative or friend. There are no dues or fees for S-Anon membership; we are self-supporting through our own contributions. S-Anon is not allied with any sect, denomination, politics, organization or institution; does not wish to engage in any controversy; neither endorses nor opposes any causes. Our primary purpose is to recover from the effects upon us of another person's sexaholism and to help families and friends of sexaholics.

THE TWELVE STEPS OF S-ANON

❧

1. We admitted we were powerless over sexaholism—that our lives had become unmanageable.

2. Came to believe that a Power greater than ourselves could restore us to sanity.

3. Made a decision to turn our will and our lives over to the care of God *as we understood Him.*

4. Made a searching and fearless moral inventory of ourselves.

5. Admitted to God, to ourselves, and to another human being the exact nature of our wrongs.

6. Were entirely ready to have God remove all these defects of character.

7. Humbly asked Him to remove our shortcomings.

8. Made a list of all persons we had harmed, and became willing to make amends to them all.

9. Made direct amends to such people wherever possible, except when to do so would injure them or others.

10. Continued to take personal inventory and when we were wrong promptly admitted it.

11. Sought through prayer and meditation to improve our conscious contact with God *as we understood Him,* praying only for knowledge of His will for us and the power to carry that out.

12. Having had a spiritual awakening as the result of these Steps, we tried to carry this message to others, and to practice these principles in all our affairs.

THE TWELVE STEPS OF
ALCOHOLICS ANONYMOUS

1. We admitted we were powerless over alcohol — that our lives had become unmanageable. 2. Came to believe that a Power greater than ourselves could restore us to sanity. 3. Made a decision to turn our will and our lives over to the care of God *as we understood Him*. 4. Made a searching and fearless moral inventory of ourselves. 5. Admitted to God, to ourselves, and to another human being the exact nature of our wrongs. 6. Were entirely ready to have God remove all these defects of character. 7. Humbly asked Him to remove our shortcomings. 8. Made a list of all persons we had harmed, and became willing to make amends to them all. 9. Made direct amends to such people wherever possible, except when to do so would injure them or others. 10. Continued to take personal inventory and when we were wrong promptly admitted it. 11. Sought through prayer and meditation to improve our conscious contact with God *as we understood Him*, praying only for knowledge of His will for us and the power to carry that out. 12. Having had a spiritual awakening as the result of these Steps, we tried to carry this message to alcoholics, and to practice these principles in all our affairs.

THE TWELVE TRADITIONS OF S-ANON

℘

1. Our common welfare should come first; personal progress for the greatest number depends upon unity.

2. For our group purpose there is but one authority — a loving God as He may express Himself in our group conscience. Our leaders are but trusted servants — they do not govern.

3. The relatives of sexaholics, when gathered together for mutual aid, may call themselves an S-Anon Family Group, provided that, as a group, they have no other affiliation. The only requirement for membership is that there be a problem of sexaholism in a relative or friend.

4. Each group should be autonomous, except in matters affecting another group or S-Anon or SA as a whole.

5. Each S-Anon Family Group has but one purpose: to help families of sexaholics. We do this by practicing the Twelve Steps of S-Anon, by encouraging and understanding our sexaholic relatives, and by welcoming and giving comfort to the families of sexaholics.

6. Our S-Anon Family Groups ought never endorse, finance, or lend our name to any outside enterprise, lest problems of money, property and prestige divert us from our primary spiritual aim. Although a separate entity, we should always cooperate with Sexaholics Anonymous.

7. Every group ought to be fully self-supporting, declining outside contributions.

8. S-Anon Twelfth Step work should remain forever non-professional, but our service centers may employ special workers.

9. Our groups, as such, ought never be organized; but we may create service boards or committees directly responsible to those they serve.

10. The S-Anon Family Groups have no opinion on outside issues; hence our name ought never be drawn into public controversy.

11. Our public relations policy is based on attraction rather than promotion; we need always maintain personal anonymity at the level of press, radio, TV and films. We need guard with special care the anonymity of all S-Anon and SA members.

12. Anonymity is the spiritual foundation of all our Traditions, ever reminding us to place principles above personalities.

S-ANON TWELVE CONCEPTS
OF SERVICE

S-Anon's Twelve Concepts of Service illustrate that Twelfth Step work can be accomplished on a broad scale. The Concepts are guidelines for the World Service Office staff, the Board of Trustees, standing committees, and World Service Conference members to relate to each other and to groups.

1. The ultimate responsibility and authority for S-Anon world services belongs to the S-Anon groups.

2. The S-Anon Family Groups have delegated complete administrative and operational authority to their Conference and its service arms.

3. The Right of Decision makes effective leadership possible.

4. Participation is the key to harmony.

5. The Rights of Appeal and Petition protect minorities and assure that they be heard.

6. The Conference acknowledges the primary administrative responsibility of the trustees.

7. The trustees have legal rights while the rights of the Conference are traditional.

8. The Board of Trustees delegates full authority for routine management of the S-Anon Headquarters to its executive committees.

9. Good personal leadership at all service levels is a necessity. In the field of world service the Board of Trustees assumes the primary leadership.

10. Service responsibility is balanced by carefully defined service authority and double-headed management is avoided.

11. The World Service Office is composed of an executive director and staff members.

12. The spiritual foundation for S-Anon's world services is contained in the General Warranties of the Conference, Article 12 of the Charter.

THE GENERAL WARRANTIES OF THE CONFERENCE

In all its proceedings the World Service Conference of S-Anon shall observe the spirit of the Traditions:

1. that only sufficient operating funds, including an ample reserve, be its prudent financial principle;
2. that no Conference member shall be placed in unqualified authority over other members;
3. that all decisions be reached by discussion, vote, and whenever possible, by unanimity;
4. that no Conference action ever be personally punitive or an incitement to public controversy;
5. that though the Conference serves S-Anon, it shall never perform any act of government; and like the fellowship of S-Anon which it serves, it shall always remain democratic in thought and action.

(The Twelve Concepts of Service reprinted and adapted with permission of Al-Anon World Services, Inc. Permission to reprint and adapt the Concepts does not imply that Al-Anon is affiliated with this program. Al-Anon is a program of recovery from the effects of alcoholism. Use of this material in connection with programs which are patterned after Al-Anon, but which address other problems, does not imply otherwise.) S-Anon's Twelve Concepts of Service were formally adopted and approved at the first annual S-Anon World Service Conference January, 2004.

ARE YOU AFFECTED BY SOMEONE'S SEXUAL BEHAVIOR?

1. Have you felt hurt or embarrassed by someone's sexual conduct?

2. Have you secretly searched for clues about someone's sexual behavior?

3. Have you lied about or covered up another person's sexual conduct?

4. Have you had money problems because of someone's sexual behavior?

5. Have you felt betrayed or abandoned by someone you loved and trusted?

6. Are you afraid to upset the sexaholic for fear that he or she will leave you?

7. Have you tried to control somebody's sexual thoughts or behavior by doing things like throwing away pornography, dressing suggestively, or being sexual with them in order to keep them from being sexual with others?

8. Have you used sex to try to keep peace in a relationship?

9. Have you tried to convince yourself that someone else's sexual thoughts and behavior shouldn't bother you?

10. Have you felt that sex plays an all-consuming role in your relationship?

11. Have you doubted your attractiveness, your emotions, and your sanity?

12. Have you felt responsible for the sexual behavior of another person?

13. Have you felt angry and/or stupid for not knowing about someone's sexual acting out behavior?

14. Have you engaged in uncomfortable, unwanted, or physically dangerous sexual behavior?

15. Have you ever thought about or attempted suicide because of someone's sexual behavior?

16. Has your preoccupation with someone's sexual thoughts and behavior affected your relationships with your children, your co-workers, and/or other friends or family members?

17. Have you neglected your physical and/or emotional health while in a relationship?

18. Have you helped someone get out of jail or other legal trouble, or feared legal action as a result of his or her sexual behavior?

19. Have you blamed other people, such as friends or sexual partners, society in general, his/her job, religion, or birth family for someone's sexual behavior?

20. Have you felt confused about what is true when talking with someone about his or her sexual thoughts or behavior?

21. Have you felt alone or too ashamed to ask for help?

22. Have you avoided painful emotions by using drugs, alcohol, or food or by being too busy?

23. Have you ever felt that someone was inappropriately attracted to you or your children?

If you can answer "yes" to some of these checklist questions, you may find help in S-Anon.

INTRODUCTION

This book is a sharing of the collective experience of the S-Anon International Family Groups fellowship. It offers hope for recovery to people whose lives have been or are being affected by the sexaholism of a spouse, parent, child, other relative, friend or acquaintance. We have found that by applying the spiritual principles of the Twelve Steps to our lives, we are able to be happy and productive, whether or not the sexaholic chooses recovery. The joy we have found in our new way of life makes us want to share the experiences that have made our recovery possible.

The Twelve Steps of S-Anon, adapted from the Twelve Steps of Alcoholics Anonymous, are the heart of the S-Anon program. While the various tools of the program and the fellowship itself support our recovery, we have found that study of these Steps from an S-Anon perspective, aiming to incorporate their principles into our lives, is essential for recovering from the destructive effects of sexaholism. In this book we share our personal stories and suggestions, based on our experience, for putting these principles into practice. In the future we hope to add our experiences with the Twelve Traditions of S-Anon as well.

WHAT YOU WILL FIND IN THIS BOOK

First, for each Step, there is a description in general terms of the devastating impact the disease of sexaholism has had on our lives and a recounting of the events and realizations that led to a new way of approaching the problem and the solution. These descriptions were written by a small group of S-Anons when our fellowship was very new, and they were used for many years in a stapled booklet form called the S-Anon "Step Study Guide." We have found that these writings still hold an enormous amount of emotional truth even though years have passed.

Several member stories are also included for each Step. Most of us have found it very helpful to become aware of how others in S-Anon have applied the principles of the Steps to their lives. These stories are intended to be a sampling of S-Anon experiences. There are as many stories as there are S-Anon members, and these examples are by no means an exhaustive catalogue of our experiences with the disease of sexaholism.

Finally, having found that we all have some inner resistance to letting go of unproductive attitudes and behavior, we have included a section called "Practicing These Principles" with each Step. These sections briefly describe some of the ways we have come face to face with our resistance to change and offer ideas that have helped many of us work through our own impediments to recovery. We also present some questions suitable for individual writing, discussion with a program sponsor or friend, or discussion within the group itself. Again, these are only examples of some issues we have addressed in the course of our recovery. The issues addressed in the questions are not intended to be a complete list of all possible issues or emotions that may arise when an individual member approaches a particular Step.

WHAT YOU WILL NOT FIND IN THIS BOOK

While S-Anon's Twelve Steps are spiritually oriented, they are not based on any specific religious discipline. The designation "God" does not refer to a particular being, force or concept, but only to "God" as each of us understands that term. When members refer to their own Higher Power in the "Member Stories," their name for God has been included out of respect for their personal understanding.

If the sexaholic behaviors mentioned in this book seem in any way vague or non-specific, let us reassure you that we are not avoiding the reality of any individual experience. No matter what manifestation of sexaholism you may have encountered in a relative or friend — be it sexual affairs with women or men, sex with children in or outside of the family, sex with animals, sex with prostitutes or other strangers, telephone sex or other use of the electronic media, compulsive use of pornography or masturbation, fantasy, voyeurism, exhibitionism, masochism, sadism, sexual violence, withholding sex, or something else — we assure you that you are not alone. When you talk with S-Anon members, you will find others who have lived with the same types of sexaholic behavior and have experienced similar feelings or reactions to sexaholism. Even if you feel unique in your local S-Anon group, you can be certain that someone in the S-Anon fellowship has also had similar experiences and feelings.

In S-Anon we consider sexaholic behaviors to be symptoms of a disease — unacceptable actions taken by sick people who are powerless over lust. Through working the S-Anon program, many of us have overcome powerful feelings of shame or guilt that arose out of being so closely connected to this "shameful" disease. We have come to understand and accept that we are not responsible for the actions of others and that those burdens of shame and guilt are not rightfully ours to carry. Our solution depends on keeping focused on our own personal path of recovery and allowing the sexaholic to do the same.

TO THOSE WHO ARE AT RISK FOR SEXUALLY TRANSMITTED DISEASES OR VIOLENCE

Everyone has the right to be safe from harm, no matter what the circumstances. Sexual contact with others can expose the sexaholic to diseases that are incurable and even fatal; in some cases these diseases can then be passed on to the sexaholic's spouse or partner and even to children through pregnancy. Sometimes partners of sexaholics are coerced into participating in unwanted sexual activities, and such activities may even be part of a pattern of domestic violence that includes physical abuse.

Members of S-Anon who found themselves in a sexual situation or a life situation that felt unsafe or even life-threatening report that it was sometimes necessary to make tough choices to protect themselves and their children. It requires tremendous courage, but the experience of those who faced these situations and were at risk for sexually transmitted diseases or violence suggest that those in similar circumstances consider taking some or all of the following actions: ask a doctor for tests for sexually transmitted diseases and follow the doctor's advice on self-protection in the future. Remember that a negative test result does not prevent a person from contracting a sexually transmitted disease from sexual contact after the test is done. Limit or abstain from sexual contact with the sexaholic for as long as necessary to maintain personal safety and recovery. Arrange with a friend, relative, or neighbor for a safe haven to go to on short notice. Obtain the phone number of an agency that can provide immediate assistance and a safe place to go. Leave money and an extra set of car keys in a place where they are readily available; and if necessary, call for police protection.

USING OTHER RESOURCES

Many members, even those who have been active in other Twelve Step programs, have found that placing the focus on ourselves in S-Anon recovery can sometimes lead to crises in relationships or the surfacing of some painful personal issues. While we believe S-Anon to be invaluable and consistently helpful over time, many in our fellowship have also sought the assistance of professional helpers like therapists, clergy, or doctors to help handle crisis situations or to deal in depth with personal issues. S-Anon does not claim to be all things to all people, and we are grateful for the specialized help available from others. The S-Anon program offers a way of living based on the Twelve Steps that is applicable in all life situations, as well as the support of people who know first-hand what the newcomer is going through because we have been there, too. This is the healing power of S-Anon. You are not alone. Recovery is possible. We invite you to join us in our common cause.

STEP ONE

❧

We admitted we were powerless over sexaholism— that our lives had become unmanageable.

We are concerned with two principles in Step One: that we cannot control the sexaholic or his or her sexual behavior, and that because of our attempts to do so our lives have become unmanageable.

Accepting our powerlessness is our first admission that we "give up." This may feel defeating and very frightening at first. In the past, we depended upon ourselves to get through every crisis or difficulty. We relied on our intellects, our theologies, our past experiences, and on new schemes and strategies we developed. We felt sure that each new strategy would work, and even when it didn't, we just bounced back with even more self-sufficiency and determination to succeed the next time. Our natural impulses were to take over, to force the issue, to make changes. We perceived ourselves to be more competent than the sexaholic and felt sure that being "strong" was the answer.

When sexaholism persisted, we began to feel that we were chasing a snowball downhill. We suffered from heartbreaks, crises, and emotional and physical ailments. Either we blamed the sexaholic for all these things or we blamed ourselves. We believed that if we were only stronger or smarter or sexier, we could somehow control the sexaholic and solve our problems.

In the meantime, those problems mounted. For many of us, unmanageability meant we were unable to adequately carry out our routine responsibilities, such as keeping the checkbook balanced, remembering appointments, keeping up with the housework, concentrating on our jobs, caring for our children, and eating and exercising properly. For others, unmanageability meant illness, substance abuse, debt, unemployment and even violence aimed at ourselves or others. We reached bottom and came to S-Anon desperate to rebuild our lives.

We had learned to be reactors rather than responders in our relationships. Some of us had taken part in the sexaholic's activities in an attempt to hold the relationship together; others had lectured and scolded in vehement opposition. Some of us had cried and pleaded and asked for promises. Others had suffered quietly, hoping and praying, afraid to tell anyone about the problem. Many of us had tried all of the above.

We became preoccupied, even obsessed, with the sexual behavior of another person. We were suspicious and tried to catch the sexaholic practicing the addiction. Some of us denied the problem, refusing to acknowledge to ourselves or others the source of our guilt, fear, and confusion. We isolated ourselves from those closest to us in an attempt to keep our secrets. We suffered fear, anxiety, depression, guilt, loneliness, rage and a lack of energy and motivation.

In S-Anon we come to realize that just as we did not cause the sexaholic's acting out, we cannot "cure" it either. We learn that it is not our responsibility to keep the sexaholic sexually sober. Instead, it is our job to manage our own lives, whether or not the sexaholic chooses sobriety.

It helped to learn that the sexaholic is suffering from a spiritual and emotional illness, and it helped to learn that we can lovingly detach from that illness. Most of all, it helped to learn that we, too, are suffering from an illness, one that can drive us to unconsciously seek out rejection, victimization, and heartache.

We slowly started to come out of our denial and isolation, and we were able to admit that there was something wrong in our homes and our relationships. We could no longer try to right those wrongs ourselves, so we came for help. Only through this utter surrender do we find strength. Our human will power cannot break the bonds of compulsive behavior, but our admission of powerlessness lays a firm foundation upon which to build our lives.

As we begin to devote ourselves to Twelve Step recovery, an amazing thing takes place. We let our hardships and problems become our teachers, and we become grateful for the lessons they teach us. We learn we are not alone in facing the problem of sexaholism. We accept the help of the group and the help of a Higher Power. We allow that Power, far greater than ourselves, to come to our aid, and we find hope.

As we begin to recover in S-Anon, we learn how to manage our lives in a way much better than ever before. We become willing to accept responsibility for our own lives, and we begin to achieve our goals. We replace our dependence on others with a dependence on God. As we begin to hold still, we feel a Higher Power begin to offer us guidance and peace in every situation. The strife and battle ceases. There is relaxation and peace, and we find serenity and dignity within ourselves.

•   •   •

M y first husband left me for a younger woman, leaving me with a sense of personal failure. I decided that my mistake had been marrying a man with "poor values" — alcoholism, materialism, and  bizarre sexual preferences. So I decided to find someone who shared my moral values: my second husband was a minister who seemed to be smart, fun, honest, thoughtful, and kind.

Four years into our marriage I became painfully aware of a passionate affair he was having. I asked myself, "How could this be? He is so different from my first husband." I was sure somehow I was wrong, so I rationalized and made it a practice to trust — and not to look for things I didn't want to see. I tried to make things better, to focus on the kids, to stick with it and try to work things out. I channeled my discomfort about my marriage into resentment, anger and criticism of issues at work, in my community and in politics. That approach worked fairly well for the next four years or so. One day, it stopped working.

There were too many suspicious lunches, notes, telephone calls, night meetings and an eerie absence even when we seemed to be most intimate. Finally my jealousy and a sense that I was competing for affection against an elusive other lover burst through my facade. I was tired of always having to keep my guard up, of competing and always losing. It was eating away at my sense of who I was, depleting what little I had left. I finally gave up. I knew that to save myself, he had to go. So I confronted him, and when I saw panic cloud his face, I knew I had been right all along. I raged and told him to get out. I couldn't live this way any more. I was screaming and throwing rocks in the middle of the night in our front yard. The unmanageability of my life lay in our rock-strewn lawn.

In the morning he asked that we make an appointment with a marriage counselor, just to help us through the separation process and to protect our son from unnecessary pain. I agreed, looking forward to the end of the madness. At that appointment the counselor confronted my husband with his sexaholism. She also confirmed my powerlessness, saying that he had to choose to get better; there was nothing I could do to change him. She suggested that he attend SA and I attend S-Anon, and I am forever grateful for that suggestion. My husband clung to his new program and I immediately grabbed hold of mine. It was a confirmation of all I had experienced — I wasn't crazy. The lasting gift of this program for me, though, has been my renewed sense of purpose and joy in myself, the knowledge that I can not only survive, but joyfully live with or without my husband. Today I use the program to live, not just live with sexaholism, and for that I am grateful.

•   •   •

I came to S-Anon based on a clear ultimatum from my wife — make some changes now or she was leaving. Despite her recovery and sexual sobriety and my attendance at meetings of another Twelve Step fellowship, according to her, our lives were still "unmanageable." I didn't know what unmanageability she was talking about, but on the advice of a counselor and people in other fellowships, I started attending S-Anon meetings.

I felt uncomfortable attending meetings at first, all these women and very few, if any, men. How could I relate to them or them to me? Slowly, as I became willing to listen and not judge, I heard pieces of my own story — the need to "fix," the feeling that everything was my fault, the resentment toward the sexaholic. What really amazed me was seeing some members, still living with active addiction, who seemed to be able to find serenity when I had none.

The unmanageability in my life became apparent to me only after months of going to meetings. I painfully began to see how I created unmanageability when I tried to control my wife, my bosses at work, the mortgage, our finances, my children's behavior — all things over which I had no control. I saw how I took responsibility for things that I had no responsibility for, and, in turn, abdicated the role that truly was mine with those people and things. In one instance after another — no matter how big or how small — I fell into the same pattern.

For example, my wife could ask, "Did you see my glasses?" and I would rage inside as I searched the house for them, wondering why she thought this was my responsibility, my problem to solve. (I seemed to miss the fact that she was simply asking a question and didn't blame me for losing the glasses. I didn't see that I was the one putting blame on myself.) Or she might want to sit down to discuss needed home improvements, but my fear of making the wrong decision would set in, and I would turn over all the plans to her. Later I would criticize (and, oh, how I could criticize!) or question the choices, which always led to an argument. I was a master at pointing out flaws and pitfalls, pointing a massive finger at the problems of life and others in my life, yet never seeing my responsibility in these problems, too.

S-Anon has taught me to stop pointing fingers and to look at myself. Is my life still unmanageable? When it is, I go back to the First Step and surrender by admitting my powerlessness over whatever it is I'm trying to control.

•   •   •

I grew up in a family saturated with the effects of sexaholism. My father had multiple affairs and attempted to sexually abuse my aunt when she was 15 years old. My parents allowed another family to live with us for the first year of my life. I believe I was sexually abused by this family friend during that time. Starting at about age 10, I was molested by the family eye doctor, who happened to be a childhood buddy of my father. This abuse continued until I entered recovery, well into adulthood, and recognized the doctor's inappropriate touching as abuse. My mother had no clue to any of this, perhaps because she was so overwhelmed by living with active sexaholism.

I began dating at age 16 when I was a junior in high school. I married when I was 27 years old. During the intervening eleven years, I was involved in seven significant relationships, each with a very different man. Underlying my dating was the belief that if only I could find *the* relationship and somehow "get it right this time," I would be happy. Not surprisingly, these relationships were all with sexaholics, and while their acting out ran the gamut from affairs with other women to compulsive masturbation, each relationship made my life unmanageable. Amazingly, I failed to recognize a pattern when these sexual problems cropped up each time.

Each relationship cost me dearly. Some of the problems I encountered included missing time from college and graduate school and not completing my assignments and job tasks. This was due to my preoccupation with the relationship and being distracted by problems the relationship created. I allowed these men to use my cars, my apartments, my food, phone, drugs, body, and time. I paid for gas and car repairs for which I was not responsible. I became involved in their projects and lives, while losing myself and my life. I bought and wore clothes solely to please them. I wasted hours of time sitting in my parked car waiting for him to come out of "her" apartment. I was fired from two jobs due to my preoccupation. I was beaten up by one man — my head bashed into a wall and my throat choked. With another man I became pregnant and agreed to have an abortion. In each relationship, I put myself at risk of catching a life-threatening sexually transmitted disease, but I ignored this fact and put my head in the sand. I contemplated suicide three times and attempted it once. My crying at work prompted co-workers to introduce me to my first Twelve Step fellowship and my own recovery process. A year later my husband identified his sexaholism and I came to S-Anon.

My life prior to S-Anon was truly unmanageable. It took many months of recovery to discover my own likes and dislikes and to quit trying to "motivate" my husband and others into action. Today my bills are paid on time. I take care of myself and give myself appropriate rest and nutrition. While life is not perfect, I am grateful for the gifts of the program. Healing and serenity have progressively grown in my heart and in my home. I can laugh, and I enjoy waking up each morning. My husband and I are happy, so are my children. I know I am powerless over other people and the choices they make, particularly my husband and his choices — even in his sobriety. Today I know that the only person I can change is me with the help of my Higher Power. These are just some of the many gifts of this program that I have received and for which I can never be sufficiently grateful.

•　　•　　•

I remember one rough period when I just couldn't seem to do anything to make my husband happy. I didn't know at the time that an affair he was having was breaking up. I just knew that he was angry with me. Underneath I felt that something was wrong, but I just tried to cope by accepting him with his quirks.

As time went on, though, I became more and more suspicious that he was seeing another woman. My own "acting out" really started to pick up then. I went through his wallet, his car, and checked up on things. I discovered the name of the person with whom he was involved. When I found out that my husband had taken our three-year-old son to her home, I even questioned my child and found out where she lived. I went to her house expecting my husband to be there and, indeed, caught him trimming her lawn. My denial was so strong that I believed him when he told me she was just a good friend, but I got suspicious again when I was in the hospital giving birth to our second child. His parents remarked that he was coming home rather late, and then I remembered that the woman he had the affair with lived across the street from the hospital. When I got out of the hospital, I alleviated the devastating pain by checking up again. I hired detectives to give me hard evidence that he could not deny. My obsession was so great that the detectives said, "Don't snoop anymore. You're going to ruin things for us!" But I couldn't stop.

I continued to focus so much on his sexaholic behavior that I couldn't pay as much attention to my children as I should have. For example, one time my son wanted to go to the pool, but I was expecting the detectives to call. I told my son we had to wait. To pass time he innocently began singing a song, but in my obsession, his singing drove me crazy. I just lost it, grabbed him and screamed at him to stop.

My unmanageability was growing, so I confronted my husband and served him with divorce papers. I couldn't tolerate the relationship any more. But he begged me to stay. I gave him a bottom line: "If we are going to stay together, we're going to see a couples counselor, you're going to cut up your credit cards, I am going to give you an allowance, you are going to call me before you leave work and I'm going to give you a reasonable amount of time to get home."

My efforts to control the situation seemed to go O.K. at first, but after five months I started getting suspicious again. I called the detectives and found out my husband had saved up his allowance for weeks and had gone to a motel with the other woman at lunch time. I finally realized that I couldn't control him. I despaired; I didn't know what to do. It was then that my Higher Power entered our lives in the form of a person who helped us find the SA and S-Anon fellowships.

I came to S-Anon hoping to find answers. I wanted to know the statistics on his chances of acting out again and how soon it was going to be. Though I didn't find statistics, I did find a supportive group who gave me unconditional love, acceptance and understanding. At a gut level they understood my situation like no one else could — not the therapist I was seeing, not my sisters, not my friends. I was in so much pain, and I was so angry. The group helped me to see that I cannot control a sexaholic's behavior and that I am powerless over *trying* to control him. Today, with the help of this fellowship and the Twelve Steps, I am happy. I am grateful to have this program and to be in this relationship with a recovering sexaholic. I also am excited and hopeful for the futures of my children, perhaps the ultimate recipients of what I'm doing today.

•   •   •

When I first came to S-Anon, I could readily admit my unmanageability. I was working two jobs because most of my husband's income went to support his sexual acting out or to one new business scheme after another. Even though my husband had lost interest in me sexually, and I knew he was sexually active with other women, I was still desperately trying to get pregnant. I frequently had "rage attacks" where I would follow him around the house or even outside screaming — and I couldn't stop. Often my anger leaked out at co-workers through sarcasm or a very cold, angry tone of voice. When I was confronted with this, I was totally surprised and hurt. How could anyone perceive me this way? I felt I was a very sensitive and caring person. The most blatant sign of my unmanageability was that I was suicidal. I vacillated between praying for my husband to die and praying that I would die. Eventually, I stayed with praying for me to die. I would go to bed each night praying not to wake up. At times I would get into the car in a hysterical rage at two or three o'clock in the morning, trying to get the nerve to drive into a wall.

In spite of the awareness of my unmanageability, it took at least six months in the S-Anon program before I accepted that I was powerless over sexaholism. I don't think I ever felt responsible for my husband's acting out, but I did feel that I was capable of curing and fixing it. When I worked evenings, I would take the telephones with me. I thought I was helping — that this would prevent him from engaging in telephone sex. I searched through his wallet, his pockets and his desk drawers hoping to find clues to his acting out. I participated in degrading and humiliating sexual activities in an attempt to gain his sexual interest and to keep him from acting out with other women. I was obsessed with him and totally out of touch with my own needs and feelings.

The unmanageability of being married to a sexaholic brought me to S-Anon. In meetings, though, I came to recognize that it was actually my mother's sexaholism that had affected me initially. My mother had many affairs before I was born and shortly after. She was also incestuous with my brother. My brother sexually abused me, and I was sexually abused by an older man when I was 18 years old. Although these facts about my family background and my childhood were very painful to face, I am grateful for the knowledge. In S-Anon I came to realize that it wasn't just bad luck that I married a sexaholic — I was being groomed for it all my life.

Over time, through the help of my S-Anon friends and my Higher Power, I was able to accept my powerlessness over sexaholism. I was able to see the difference between being powerless and being helpless. I recognized my powerlessness over sexual addiction and my own crazy thinking and behavior. I saw I was not helpless to take positive action to face my pain. With this admission, I really started to work the First Step and my own program.

PRACTICING
THESE
PRINCIPLES

❧

We found that regardless of how the sexaholic acted out, our feelings were often quite similar. We experienced anger, disbelief, humiliation, betrayal, fear, anxiety, depression, hopelessness, guilt and numbness, to name just a few. In Step One we saw that our attempts to control or deny, so often driven by these powerful emotions, resulted in unman- ageability in virtually every aspect of our lives. Paradoxically, it was our surrender, our admission of complete lack of power over the sexaholic and sexaholism, that laid the foundation for the serenity this program of recovery offers.

Step One reminds us of our proper relationship with others — we are powerless over them. It places us in correct relationship with ourselves — when we try to control others, we lose the ability to manage our own lives. Step One is the true beginning of our path to recovery.[1]

It was difficult for most of us to make the transition from focusing on the behavior of the sexaholic to focusing on the ways in which our reactions to sexaholism contributed to the unmanageability of our lives. This gradual shift in focus, however, is an essential process that, while often painful at first, is the key to beginning our recovery. Many of us had to ask our Higher Power to

---

[1] *Paths to Recovery: Al-Anon's Steps, Traditions and Concepts*, page 10.

help us cultivate attitudes of honesty, open-mindedness, and willingness to admit that our efforts to cope with sexaholism had failed.

Most of us found that reflecting upon and writing about questions like the following, as well as questions in *The S-Anon Checklist* (see p. xiii), were helpful as we honestly examined our experience. While there is no requirement to share these thoughts, many of us benefitted from sharing our reflections with a sponsor, other program members or our group. Upon completing our First Step, some of us also made a commitment to ourselves and our sponsor about what behavior we would practice, as well as avoid, to be "sober" in our S-Anon program. We also made a commitment to use the tools of the S-Anon program described in Conference-Approved Literature, such as meetings, sponsorship, sharing with S-Anon members, and service within the fellowship. We kept in mind, however, that we are striving for "progress, not perfection."

• • •

STEP ONE

We admitted we were powerless over sexaholism — that our lives had become unmanageable.

∞ What people or situations fit the following for me: "If only _____ were different, my life would be better." Have I tried to change these people or situations? What was the result?

∞ For what behaviors of others have I felt responsible?

❧ What have been the consequences in my life (emotional, physical, mental, sexual, spiritual, social, occupational, financial) of my attempts to control or deny sexaholism?

❧ What are the themes and patterns of my attempts to control or deny? What behaviors do I keep returning to, even though they keep producing the same unsatisfying result? Where did I learn these behaviors? What are the situations or behaviors in others that tend to provoke my predictable reactions?

❧ What does it mean for me to be "powerless over sexaholism?" By admitting my powerlessness, what do I surrender? What do I have the power to change?

❧ Have I avoided focusing on my own needs or conduct by placing my focus on the sexaholism of someone else? What needs of my own have I ignored? What personal behavior is difficult for me to acknowledge?

❧ What is the history of my relationships with significant others? As I look at these relationships, do any patterns become apparent?

❧ What would it mean for me to be "sober" in S-Anon? What program tools can I use to maintain my sobriety?

STEP TWO

❧

*Came to believe
that a Power
greater than ourselves
could restore us
to sanity.*

A dmitting our powerlessness may make us feel defeated, but it is really the first step toward rebuilding our lives. We now know we need help. Who will give it to us and how can we get it?

Only a Higher Power can remove our obsessiveness; however, what if we don't believe or what if we had a religion when we were children and it didn't work? S-Anon is not a religious program. It is a spiritual program of suggested Steps that lead us to new insights and growth. We need only admit that we are not the greatest power in the universe and that we have been unable to solve our problems alone.

Admitting we can't do it alone is difficult for a person who believes he or she is intellectually self-sufficient. In fact, we often made our own intellect our God, believing that by reason and sheer will we could solve our own problems. We were humbled by sexaholism, and those of us who had no faith when we entered the program are beginning to find it here. At first some of us turned to our S-Anon group as our Higher Power, listening for the truth spoken through the people and the principles of the Twelve Steps.

Those of us who already believed might have thought that we knew all about God and that we might tell the group a thing or two about Him. We soon learn true humility, which shows us that God's presence and wisdom is found in the S-Anon fellowship. We find our faith deepening as we surrender the parts of ourselves we have always held back from God. We are finally willing to start on the journey of truly knowing ourselves. Many of us have yet to experience a spiritual awakening, but we are committed to taking the Steps of this program with an open, seeking mind. We know we are on the right path.

In Step One we learn that we are powerless over sexaholism and that our lives have become unmanageable, but we are not left alone. A Power greater than ourselves can restore us to sanity. What is this restoration to sanity we talk about?

Haven't we acted irrationally at times trying to deal with our relationships? We tried checking up on the sexaholic all over town, using tranquilizers and liquor to calm our frazzled nerves, and obsessing over the sexaholic instead of tending to ourselves. We became hysterical. We cried, screamed, nagged, and threatened over and over again, all of which we thought was doing something about the problem.

Now we can really do something! We can trust God to do what we cannot do for ourselves. Trust is an ingredient of believing, and to believe is to actively pursue the thing hoped for.

Many of us believed at first that the only way to rise above our problems was to run away from them. We learned that a geographical move was not the answer. We have to make a spiritual move, or face the prospect of repeating our pattern of choosing unhealthy relationships. We need to face reality and learn how to accept it. We need to begin our own recovery, apart from the sexaholic's. Physically or emotionally running away only prolongs the pain. We see that we do have a way out; we have options and choices we can make for our own lives. With every hardship we face, our Higher Power also provides an outlet. One of those ways out is to change our own attitudes with the help of our Higher Power and the S-Anon program.

In seeing our need for a Higher Power, we realize that it is safe for us to be dependent upon God; however, it is risky to depend exclusively for our well-being on another human being. We all have a hunger which we call the "God hunger." We attempt to satisfy this hunger with a relationship with another person when we are really looking for a Higher Power. We can go to that Higher Power for refuge and strength. We also have the support, encouragement and understanding that we gain when we share with one another.

It is startling and humbling to realize that we are often as addicted as the sexaholic. We may not be addicted to sex or substances, but sometimes we are addicted to people and situations in our lives. Ours is no less serious an addiction; in some cases we've suffered as devastatingly from our addiction as the sexaholic has. We need the help of a Power greater than ourselves to bring us back to sanity.

It is important to remember to be patient with ourselves during this process of being restored to sanity. We are not asked to do all this at once. It takes time to develop faith and to recover. Feeling guilty and having expectations of a quick recovery only interferes with the healing process.

> We never apologize to anyone for depending upon our Creator. We can laugh at those who think spirituality the way of weakness. Paradoxically, it is the way of strength. The verdict of the ages is that faith means courage. All men of faith have courage. They trust their God. We never apologize for God. Instead, we let Him demonstrate, through us, what He can do.[2]

•   •   •

---

[2] *Alcoholics Anonymous*, p. 68

Step Two
STORIES

My parents were not religious at all, and I was brought up with more of an ethnic and cultural identity than a religious one. When I met the man I would marry, I found that his family was much more religiously-oriented than mine; his brother was even a religious leader. My husband wanted us to follow religious teachings and so I agreed to do that. We had four children and taught them the principles of our faith. We even sent them to religious school for education. We followed the tenets and were a "religious family."

Then sexaholism broke through all the boundaries of our religion and came full force into our home. My view of religion became very negative and I was angry. I had participated in religious activities in order to be a "good wife" and not create problems, yet this disease had brought insanity into our home.

I was still feeling angry when I started going to S-Anon meetings. In my group there was an older woman who seemed very different than me and who talked about God and how important God was to her. She would say in the meetings time and time again to "hit your knees." Whenever she said that, I wanted to leave because I was not about to have anything to do with God. I kept coming to meetings, but I wouldn't sit next to her.

I went on for many months rejecting the "God part" of the program. I would walk in the mornings and recite the Twelve Steps. I would go to meetings almost nightly, but I would not accept that there was a power greater than myself. One day as I was walking and obsessing about a hypothetical conversation that might or might not ever happen, it occurred to me that even though I didn't believe in God, I could call a higher being "HP." I felt fairly comfortable with that. Even though I was doubtful that HP could do anything for me, I began visualizing a little gnome sitting on my left shoulder. This little shoulder gnome was with me all the time and believed in me. When my thoughts became too terrifying for me, I talked to the little gnome and I felt better. It took another six or seven months before I took that woman's suggestion and "hit my knees." I remember that morning and the relief I felt by taking the action of going to my knees. I knew then that I, too, could have a God of my understanding who would be with me and help me. In my Step Two process I became acutely aware that religion and spirituality were not the same, and I could believe in God as I have come to understand God. That is a comforting thought for me.

• • •

The only word I noticed in Step Two for a very long time was "sanity." It stood out like a neon billboard, blocking the "came to believe" part. Why was that word there? What did it mean? The word "restore" suggested I had been sane at one time or another. Before I could actively pursue sanity, and come to believe God could and would restore me to sanity, I had to have a clear understanding of what the word meant for me.

There was not much in my current life, or in my childhood filled with abandonment and neglect, to indicate what sanity was or how to get it. I had learned to adapt to others as the way to survive, almost totally losing myself in the process. "Shoulds" and "oughts" sprinkled my vocabulary and guided my thinking. I was very busy mothering and managing other people. I spent all my time trying to figure out how to make them happy, while denying my own needs. Since this was all I knew, this seemed sane to me. As the disease of sexaholism progressed, though, my life and my family's lives became more unmanageable. I felt deserted by the God who had sustained me as a child.

One day while watching small children play, I realized they were the healthiest, most sane people I knew. They knew how to live life in the present. They had trust and did not question the fact they were cared for by a greater power. They knew they could not do it all alone and did not hesitate to ask for help or reassurance. They let go of pain and hurts easily. They definitely had lives of their own and had no false shame. They liked and enjoyed being themselves and were eager to learn and grow on their own. They had confidence in what they had learned so far and were willing to take risks to live. They were behaving appropriately for their ages. What a picture of sanity! This was something I could believe in and pursue. Now I have a checklist for my unhealthy thinking. I can strive to bring the healthy attitudes expressed by those children into my adult life. This is sanity and God's will for me. What a difference this has made in my life!

•   •   •

I was vaguely aware that my reaction to my husband's behavior was crazy. Sometimes when my partner seemed especially critical and mean-spirited, I would become depressed and hopeless and would ask God for help and comfort. Twice my pleas for help were followed by discovery of evidence of my partner's affairs. I came face to face with the truth about my situation; my denial was broken. On both occasions I felt that God was bringing those facts to light, but I was afraid of the truth, and I was upset that God would answer my call for help with more pain. Therefore, I made excuses for the betrayals and tried harder to manage my life without God's help.

Living with the effects of sexaholism wore me out, and I finally reached the limits of my own power. I realized that I could not solve my problems without help. I had no other options, so I turned to God once more. This time it was with a different attitude. I said a prayer that went something like this: "God, I can't take it anymore. I need your help. I realize that in the past you have answered my prayers with some painful truths. If there is more pain to go through in order to stop my suffering, then I'm willing to accept it, whatever the cost."

Following the prayer, I asked my husband to level with me about the other women. Instead of the standard denial and counter-attack, he admitted everything. As I had feared, it was painful to face the truth, but in doing so I began laying the foundation for the serenity I would come to find.

It has been over ten years since the day I first came to believe that God could, and would, restore me to sanity. I had feared that facing the truth would mean the end of my relationship with my partner, but it turned out to be just the beginning. With God's help and some time, the wounds healed. I no longer turn to God only in a crisis. I apply God's will to the little things in life as well, like struggles at work. I've learned that frustration is a sign that I have lost sight of Step Two — that I am relying on my own plan and power instead of God's plan and God's power. The program slogans "Turn it Over" and "Let Go and Let God" remind me that there is a Higher Power. Each time I practice these slogans, I come to believe on a deeper level.

•   •   •

Step Two for me has been like the bigger-and-bigger hammer theory exemplified in the old Bugs Bunny cartoons. Bugs hits Daffy Duck over the head with a hammer, only the hammer is the size of a gavel, insufficient to get Daffy's attention. By the time all is said and done, Bugs is whamming Daffy with a mallet the size of a family car.

In an exaggerated and humorous way, this cartoon reminds me of how my Higher Power lovingly tried to reach me my whole life. Even though I grew up in a very religious family, my ego thrived as my personal god well into my adulthood. Consequently I did not have a real relationship with God. Instead, my attention was focused on controlling my own life and manipulating other peoples' lives. The little gavels of life didn't work on me. It took a huge "hammer" to get through to me — the crisis of sexaholism in my home — before I could understand the need for a Higher Power in my life.

My husband told me about his disease — a disclosure based on fear of arrest. During the next six weeks I exhausted myself in an insane effort to single-handedly manage the situation. Questions raced through my brain: Who would be the best therapist for him? Which lawyer would be most effective? Who could we call at the newspapers if any of this threatened to come out? I felt as if I was running faster and faster on a hamster wheel and life was just a blur. It was at this, my lowest point, that my Higher Power seemed to step in and say what I could not: "Enough!" My denial was stripped away by blunt revelations in a joint therapy session. I was overwhelmed by the enormity of sexaholism, and I finally realized my powerlessness. It became clear that the consequences of my husband's sexaholic actions were not for me to control. It had been insane for me to think I could. For the first time, I became aware in a real way that my Higher Power would take charge of the situation, if only I was willing to believe.

When I faced this crisis — perhaps the deepest crisis of my life — and reached a rock-bottom emptiness, I finally was able to feel and accept my Higher Power's presence in my life. The crisis caused my youthful understanding of God to begin to give way to a deeper, personal, spiritual experience and understanding. I am grateful that my early religious training laid a foundation for me by giving me a concept of a Higher Power. I'm even more grateful that in this program I have come to know a God who really cares for me, who has a better plan for my life than the one I have in mind.

PRACTICING
THESE
PRINCIPLES

❧

In Step One we finally accepted that we could not recover alone, but who could help us out of the emptiness created when we admitted our own powerlessness over sexaholism? At this point, some of us were tempted to fill the void with people, activities or even substances, but we found only a real Higher Power could truly help us. We were relieved to discover that Step Two suggested only that we admit that we were not the greatest power in the universe.

> *...we may be powerless, but we are not helpless, and we are not alone.*[3]

That recognition laid the foundation for "coming to believe" — a process of becoming aware of the presence of a Higher Power in our lives.

Some of us had preconceived ideas about God that stood in our way, particularly if we had been hurt by people whose religious attitudes were controlling or punishing. Others were uneasy about the differing spiritual views of group members. However, if our old ideas about God, religion or spirituality had not worked well for us in the past, we were encouraged to begin a new relationship with the Higher Power of our own understanding. In this regard it helped some of us to recognize that we had allowed our spiritual lives to stagnate in the turmoil of trying to deal with sexaholism, so it was not surprising that our understanding of God had not kept up with our growth in other areas of our lives. The wisdom of the

---

[3] *Paths to Recovery: Al-Anon's Steps, Traditions and Concepts*, p. 18.

ages seems to agree that it is not only all right, but necessary to develop and maintain a concept of God that meets our changing understanding of ourselves and our world, as long as it is a Power greater than ourselves. Through our growing trust in this Higher Power, sanity is restored in our lives, and we move toward peace, serenity, and useful lives.

Those of us who resisted the idea that we needed to be "restored to sanity" were encouraged to return to our First Step writing and remind ourselves of the many ways in which our lives had become unmanageable. Many of us even found that after weeks or months of listening to the experience of others in meetings, we became aware at a deeper level of our own powerlessness over sexaholism and the need for a Higher Power to restore us.

•   •   •

STEP TWO

Came to believe that a Power greater than ourselves
could restore us to sanity.

❧ Have I looked to the sexaholic to satisfy my "God-hunger?" How have I tried to fill this void in other unhealthy ways?

❧ What are the things I keep doing over and over again expecting different results? In what situations have I been unable to perceive reality clearly? What does it mean to be restored to sanity?

❧ How have I understood God in the past? Who or what in my life did this God of my understanding resemble (for example, a parent, a religious leader, etc.)? What obstacles, if any, does my understanding of God present for me in accepting help from a

Higher Power? What part of this understanding, which may have been influenced by others, do I accept, reject or remain undecided on?

ക Have I considered asking my Higher Power to help and guide my efforts to come to an understanding of God? Do I have anything to lose if I try?

ക Reflecting on the experiences of others in the group, how do I see a Higher Power working in *my* life today? What have I learned in the S-Anon program that gives me hope for the future?

ക In Step Three we turn our will and our life over to the care of God, *as we understand Him*. Part of Step Two is determining how we understand our Higher Power. In working this Step and preparing for Step Three, some of us wrote down our answer to the following: "What is my understanding or concept of God today?"

ക It has been said that a relationship is a two-way street. What are some things I can do to begin developing a relationship with the Higher Power of my understanding?

STEP THREE

❧

Made a decision
to turn our will and
our lives over
to the care of God
as we understood Him.

U ntil now, we may have believed that the sexaholic and our own compulsive concerns were the only things we needed to turn over to God. Now we are called upon to surrender our will and our lives, to surrender ourselves completely. This is difficult for all of us, but haven't we already begun this process by relying on our S-Anon group or maybe our sponsor? We have learned that clinging desperately to an unmanageable way of life doesn't work. It is only when we let go of our desperation that we begin to truly live our lives. We are like drowning swimmers: by struggling to save our lives, we sink even deeper; by relaxing, we float to the surface. When we are willing to give up our lives, we can truly gain them. In other words, by depending on God to do what we cannot do, we gain independence of spirit.

We are familiar with dependence; in the past we depended upon other people as our source of security, validation and comfort. We see that it does not work for us to depend emotionally and spiritually on another. Now, instead, we can depend upon a Higher Power with the strength to guide us in times of need and indecision. We can be confident that God is always there for us and always desires the greatest good for us. Anyone can begin to tap into this source. To do so, we must only be willing. In fact, the key to Step Three is the willingness to trust in a Higher Power.

We used to think we could only trust ourselves, and most of us have plenty of good reasons to have developed that philosophy. But in our current attempts to live in healthy adult relationships, we are beginning to see that our old philosophies are no longer effective. They aren't making us happy. We had been certain that our own intelligence, backed by strong will power, was the only way to control our lives. At one time it seemed like a wise policy, but it didn't pay off. We tried to play God in our own lives, with disastrous results.

We were driven to S-Anon by that near-destruction at our own hands. Self-will ran riot in our lives. Now we admit defeat, and in S-Anon we begin to acquire the faith to recover. We learn we need not face our problems alone. Instead, we learn to turn our will and our lives over to the care of God.

"*...God as we understood Him*" is an important part of Step Three. Many of us who have taken this Step certainly didn't understand very much about God in the beginning. But as we were willing to make this leap of faith, we began to believe in a God who is loving, forgiving and encouraging to us. We felt free to shed old concepts of God that made us feel "apart from" or unworthy, and we began to understand new and hopeful spiritual concepts.

As we continue to see aspects of self-will emerge, we further realize the futility of our attempts to run our own lives. We see that the myth of self-sufficiency is full of pride and that it leaves us feeling isolated and lonely. When we surrender to God, we connect with a Higher Power and become whole persons.

Some people criticize those who rely on God, accusing them of leaning on a crutch. The truth is that everyone needs some support, whether they are willing to admit it or not. Let's begin to lean on the right One for us.

Our understanding of our Higher Power is not really a matter of logic. Few of us can be reasoned or argued into faith. Belief in a wise, powerful and loving God usually comes from seeing a Higher Power at work in our own lives. To see this Power at work, we have to give God something to work with. Let's begin with ourselves.

Exactly how can we turn our wills and our lives over to God? We make a decision to conform to God's will instead of our own. We are the only ones who can make that decision. When we begin to conform to God's will, we are on the right track. "Not my will but thine be done" is the motto for Step Three. As the alcoholics put it, "Our whole trouble had been the misuse of willpower. We had tried to bombard our problems with it instead of attempting to bring it into agreement with God's intention for us."[4]

We found it helpful to take this Step with a loved one, best friend or spiritual advisor, but it is better to meet God alone in this than to do it with someone who cannot accept our understanding. Our words, of course, are up to us as long as we sincerely express our hearts.

Having the best intentions and motives for what we do is not always a guarantee we will do the right things. Simply having faith in a Higher Power is not enough. We have to surrender our will and our lives over and over again. Now, in all times of emotional disturbance and indecision we can pause, get quiet, and in that stillness let go of our problems and worries. We can have the confidence that we have an ever-present help in times of need.

This is one suggestion of how to approach the God of our understanding in Step Three:

> God, I offer myself to Thee — to build with me and to do with me as Thou wilt. Relieve me of the bondage of self, that I may better do Thy will. Take away my difficulties, that victory over them may bear witness to those I would help of Thy Power, Thy Love, and Thy Way of life. May I do Thy will always.[5]

• • •

[4] [Alcoholics Anonymous] *Twelve Steps and Twelve Traditions*, p. 40.
[5] *Alcoholics Anonymous*, p. 63.

Before I had a name for it, I felt the presence of sexaholism creeping into our home: less laughter, more criticism, lies, excuses, hostility, no eye contact and, perhaps most painful, the emotional distance in our sexual relations. I felt like I was being used rather than loved. My powerlessness over sexaholism led me to the point of despair, and it was clear I had to take some sort of action to get relief. I decided to read some Conference Approved Literature one night because I had heard it suggested at an S-Anon meeting as a method of coping with those difficult highs and lows we experience, and I was at my lowest. I picked up *Alcoholics Anonymous* (the "Big Book") and began to read it for hope and comfort. I came upon the directions for taking Step Three on page 63. Feeling like I had hit bottom and couldn't do it on my own anymore, I made a decision to let God into my life — without conditions. I prayed the Third Step prayer with a sincere attitude as it suggested. I was comforted to see that the section on the Third Step concluded with these words: "This was only a beginning, though if honestly and humbly made, an effect, sometimes a very great one, was felt at once."

Two days later I went to my S-Anon meeting. About half way through the meeting I suddenly felt a sense of peace and wholeness come over me. As I looked around the room at others, I felt my Higher Power was allowing me to see them and myself through God's eyes with God's love. I had the sense of being given a divine glimpse of myself. I saw how I had come into the meeting that night with fear, self-righteousness and superiority; how I had silently compared myself to others, judging them by their clothing, hairstyle and self-confidence. With new eyes, I now saw how this perpetual judging had created unmanageability in my life. While others were unaware of how they didn't meet my expectations, I was consumed with ensuring that the "flaws" I criticized in others would not be found in me. As I became fully aware of how my judging had primarily hurt me, it felt like that defect was lifted from me. I sat in the meeting with a changed perception of myself and others.

While the intense sense of peace and wholeness of my first, very spiritual Third Step experience has faded, the personality changes have been lasting. I am able to regain some of that peace and wholeness by working Steps Three and Eleven — turning over my life to God and seeking contact with my Higher Power daily. Today I'm aware that I did not recognize the significance of the Third Step experience while it was happening. It was a long time afterward that I fully realized the gift of grace I had been given. It may come to others more quickly or slowly, but I believe that spiritual gifts will always materialize if I work the Steps.

• • •

After working another Twelve Step program for several years, my life was filled with growth, peace, serenity and acceptance. Upon finding out about my spouse's sexaholism, it all slipped away. I had great difficulty letting go of this new issue. This, I thought, is too big, too deadly and too frightening to let go of. I was again struggling to surrender my will to my Higher Power.

When I came to S-Anon I knew my life was unmanageable, but I couldn't see how I was contributing to it. I understood Step Three in my other program, yet I didn't see that my snooping and checking up on my spouse was my way of holding on, not letting go. Even though I had experienced the fullness and freedom of knowing and accepting my powerlessness in my other program, in the area of my husband's sexaholism I was still clinging to my will — my safety and protector (or so I thought). I was too frightened to trust God with this.

In S-Anon, I learned how to detach and surrender where sexaholism was concerned. I finally came to believe — again — that it didn't matter what the story, hardship, or circumstances were. Surrendering to my Higher Power was the only way to feel calm, clear, serene, and safe. Step Three told me that I was not alone and that regardless of circumstances, I would be O.K. I could trust that my Higher Power had a plan for me that was better than I could imagine.

After being in S-Anon 18 months, I found out my spouse had been acting out the entire time he had been "in recovery." I hit a new bottom, going through depression, panic attacks, grief, and loss of the sexual intimacy I thought we had been rebuilding. Deep down I knew that Step Three was still the answer. I turned the situation over to my Higher Power, and with God's help I worked through my difficult feelings.

I am thankful for this simple program and the knowledge that no matter how difficult the challenges are, Step Three works just the same. When I risked going through my fear and once again surrendered my life to my Higher Power, I found the serenity, peace and acceptance I so badly wanted to regain. I now know on a deeper level that the God of my understanding will always be there to strengthen me if I surrender my will and my life.

•　　•　　•

I was molested in early adolescence by my grandfather. After I became aware of my husband's sexaholism and began attending S-Anon, I saw that my molestation secret needed to be shared. As I went to the meetings and called my sponsor and others, I learned to share this secret and other emotional struggles. Through this process, I found I could release some of the hurt, and I experienced healing. I eventually came to see the molestation as a part of my history. I no longer had great pain, bitterness or anger about it. Clearly, the family disease of sexaholism influenced my life, and I could use my S-Anon program to help me work on issues as they arose.

I went to meetings and listened and talked to others. I worked on willingness, and I surrendered various issues to my Higher Power, including when to share with my family about the molestation. I asked for guidance. This went on for several years. When I traveled the long distance to visit my family, I would say to myself, "This is the time to share" — but it didn't come about. So I would go back to surrendering my will. Finally, I became open to the possibility that it might not be the will of my Higher Power for this information to be revealed to my family.

Then my younger sister attempted suicide, and it was disclosed that she had been sexually abused. My Higher Power seemed to give me the "green light," and I trusted an intuition that the time was right. I made a phone call to my mom and told her I'd been sexually abused, too. She expressed great anguish, and I recognized a need for some professional help to assist our family. It was at this time that I believe my Higher Power really took care of me, guided my life and showed me that He had a broad perspective of the situation and I a narrow one. My original plan had been to tell only my parents, but now through the family therapy sessions, I would tell my two sisters and brother, too. I had thought that sharing my secret was about me and my desire for real honesty and intimacy with my family. I now began to see my Higher Power wanted those things and open communication for all members of the family. Today I'm grateful that I can trust that I will always be in the care of my Higher Power whose perspective is so much wider than my own, and that with each decision I face, I can choose His will for my life with confidence.

• • •

I remember reading Step Three and thinking "I can do this!" Making a decision felt comfortable; that is, a decision is an action, something to do. I'm much better at doing than not doing something. So I "did" Step Three; I "decided" every day, every hour, every minute, but I found no relief.

Then it was suggested that once I made the decision, I needed to let go — to surrender. "How does one let go?" I asked myself. I pictured myself holding my husband as he was dangling over the edge of a cliff. Surely letting go would not be caring or loving! To me the word "surrender" implied being forced to do something against my will. Would God force me to do something against my will? Would He expect me to abandon the one I loved? I couldn't make sense of this, and I prayed and prayed about it.

Then in a meeting, a woman shared about her "God Jar" and about how her life had become peaceful. I had seen a change in her over the months, so I asked her after the meeting to explain her "God

Jar." The idea was to write down on a piece of paper exactly what I wanted to give to God, then drop it (let go of it) into the jar. Taking the thought out of my mind and putting it on paper, then putting the piece of paper into the jar (God's hands) seemed like a helpful, visual, concrete action to me. Driving home, I began to dismiss the whole idea. When that familiar sinking sensation returned as I drove in my driveway, I decided to try the God Jar anyway. If it didn't work, I just wouldn't tell anyone. I found a large jar in a cabinet and wrote down the obsessive thoughts that were spinning in my mind about my husband's sexaholism and our marriage. I decided to let God have the situation, and I let the note fall into the jar.

I didn't expect much, but by the next morning I was pleasantly surprised by a sense of peace that I had not known before. I sat down and wrote lots of little notes to add to the jar. On New Year's Eve, seven months after I began using the God Jar, I opened the jar and read each little note. I could see that almost all my requests had been granted, but not necessarily in the way I had pictured in my mind. Rather, they had been answered completely and beautifully, in surprising and unforeseen ways. Thank God my Higher Power is bigger than my imagination!

It has been over three years since I surrendered my husband's sexaholism and surrendered our marriage to God. I didn't understand how my husband could choose to continue to act out and not seek recovery, but I had the courage and the strength to let the marriage go when it became time. Today, I am grateful to God for the gifts of that relationship, the changes that have occurred in my life, my rich relationship with my Higher Power and more people who really love me than I could ever have imagined.

PRACTICING
THESE
PRINCIPLES

❧

In Step Two we re-examined our beliefs about our Higher Power and whether or not the God of our understanding could or would restore us to sanity. It was not possible for any of us to approach Step Three unless we were at least willing to believe in a God with that kind of power. How else could we even think of turning over our will and our lives to the care of a Higher Power as called for in Step Three?

For many of us who thought we could only trust ourselves, the concept of surrender seemed truly frightening. Yet through obsessing about others' opinions and clinging to unrealistic expectations of ourselves and them, had we not essentially turned over our will and lives to the care of other people? When we

What did we have to lose by making this decision? Only our stubborn determination to have things our way; only the despair that came from repeated disappointments. And what did we gain? A new life, with purpose, meaning, and constant progress, and all the contentment and fulfillment that comes from such growth.[6]

---

[6] *Al-Anon's Twelve Steps and Twelve Traditions,* p. 21.

think back to our failed attempt to cope with sexaholism without help, do we really have anything to lose? Now we can let go of our dependence on the sexaholic, let go of our illusions of control over other people and outcomes, and, most important, let go of desperately trying to play God in our own lives.

Step Three suggests that we make a decision to surrender our lives, one day at a time, to our Higher Power, and for most of us this involved both a formal decision and a process. We first made a decision to turn over our efforts to control or ignore the sexaholism of our loved one and our reactions to it. The peace of mind and serenity that results from daily practice of this Step made us increasingly willing to surrender more and more areas of our lives until we found ourselves truly wanting to turn over our entire will and lives to the care of God as we understood God. We found that surrender was no longer a dreadful prospect, it was our freedom from mental and emotional slavery.

In taking Step Three, many of us found it helpful to reflect on the following questions and to share our reflections with a sponsor, spiritual advisor or someone else who accepts our understanding of a Higher Power.

•   •   •

STEP THREE

*Made a decision to turn our will and our lives
over to the care of God **as we understood Him**.*

☘ If I knew that a Higher Power was truly in charge of my life and that everything happening now would work out for the best, how would I feel and act? How does that differ from my current feelings and actions?

☘ What are some examples of my attempts to play God in my own life or the lives of others? What were the results?

☘ What thing, person, belief or way of life might I be "clinging to desperately?" Being rigorously honest, what am I most afraid to surrender?

☘ Have I formally taken the Third Step? If not, what is holding me back?

☘ What are things I can do to become willing to trust my Higher Power? What situations in my life could I trust to my Higher Power right now?

☘ Do I understand that Step Three is both an action Step and a daily process?

☘ How does the AA Third Step Prayer quoted in this chapter apply to me? How might I express the ideas of this prayer in my own words?

STEP FOUR

❦

Made a searching and fearless moral inventory of ourselves.

Step Four is an action Step. We do something concrete to continue our process of personal growth by looking at ourselves truthfully. We begin by examining our own character defects. This process is not so much self-analysis as it is self-examination. It is a relaxed, objective look at what's really there. It leads to self-understanding, which can help us to make great changes in our thoughts and behavior. When we search through our own moral issues, we can look deep into attitudes, motives and secret thoughts we hide so well.

As we explored the sources of our problems, the deep roots of our misery became more apparent. We discovered that we were the source of much of the pain for which we had blamed others. We examined our attitudes and behavior in a thorough way for the first time and began to see that the sexaholic wasn't the only one causing problems in the relationship. We were willing to search out, spend some time and be thorough with ourselves.

An inventory is usually a method of counting items to find what is on hand and what is missing. Step Four is similar, except that we take stock of assets and defects of character. We find that we all have qualities that are positive, some that are negative and some that are still unknown, and as we work Step Four, we shed light upon some aspects of our characters that may have been blocking our spiritual growth.

Many S-Anon members have confessed that Step Four was hard to face, but as we put our fear aside we can take up this challenge with the help of our Higher Power. As we ask for this help, we know that we won't be alone in our task. We will probably also need the help and guidance of a sponsor or another S-Anon group member with whom to share our findings.

We do not want to judge ourselves by our own standards. Neither do we want to compare ourselves with others and make excuses like "everyone does that." We do want to examine ourselves in the light we have been given by God as we understand Him and by the principles of our program.

We may find deep resentment inside for the sexaholic and all we have been through; however, as we look at our own resentful behavior, we begin to see that resentment isn't any better than lusting. It is just a different defect of character. Our own personality defects have contributed to the instability of our relationships and the chaos of our homes.

Some common symptoms of our emotional insecurity are worry, anger, self-pity and depression. We are still ultimately responsible for the way we respond to others, even if it seems that others cause these emotions inside us. To take an accurate inventory, it helps to take into consideration all the relationships that have caused recurring conflicts. We may ask ourselves questions similar to these: Looking into the past and present, what sexual or relationship situations have caused me anxiety, bitterness, or pain? Looking at each situation fairly, can I see where I have been at least partially responsible, due to either my reaction or my participation? If I am disturbed by the behavior of others, why do I lack the ability to detach with compassion? Answering these kinds of questions can disclose the source of our discomfort.

Many of our problems come from our inability to form a true partnership with another human being:

> Either we insist upon dominating the people we know, or we
> depend upon them far too much. If we lean too heavily on people,
> they will sooner or later fail us, for they are human, too, and can-
> not possibly meet our incessant demands. In this way our insecu-
> rity grows and festers. When we habitually try to manipulate

others to our own willful desires, they revolt, and resist us heavily. Then we develop hurt feelings, a sense of persecution, and a desire to retaliate. As we redouble our efforts at control, and continue to fail, our suffering becomes acute and constant. We have not once sought to be one in a family, to be a friend among friends, to be a worker among workers, to be a useful member of society. Always we tried to struggle to the top of the heap, or to hide underneath it. This self-centered behavior blocked a partnership relation with any one of those about us.[7]

Thoroughness is a key word in Step Four. It is wise to write out our questions and answers as well as our structured inventories and histories. Just thinking about our personal characteristics does not tend to be thorough or concrete, and it is too hard to remember when we are ready to work Step Five. Some of us found a suggested list of character qualities and examined ourselves within that structure. Others wrote down our life story by recording significant events from childhood on up and the feelings and thoughts we had.

It is important not to condemn ourselves and not to despair about any negative characteristics we may uncover. Most of us already suffer from excessive feelings of guilt, but all human beings have character defects. Heaping blame upon ourselves is not the way out of our difficulties. Also, let us not take the blame for what others do. As we work our program we will see that our shortcomings can become assets, and we will find serenity.

•   •   •

---

[7] [Alcoholics Anonymous] *Twelve Steps and Twelve Traditions*, p. 53.

For almost all of my first year in program, each time I read the Fourth Step I saw "Take a scrupulous and moralistic personal inventory of your spouse." In my hurt and anger I was happy to do his Fourth Step daily. Eventually my rage diminished and my eyes got sharper. I began to see more clearly, and the sexaholic began to move from the foreground of my field of vision to the background. I felt my Higher Power drawing me to the Fourth Step, and I began to peer into what seemed to be a dark emptiness — the real me.

Needing direction, I took a collection of Fourth Step formats to my sponsor, hoping she would help me choose the "right" format. She said there was no right way and that perhaps my need to do it perfectly could even be a beginning place. She stressed that it was much more important to do the inventory than it was to choose the "perfect" way. Her only requirement for me was that I could not write only about my defects, but my assets as well. She knew all too well my tendency to be too hard on myself.

I began writing about my perfectionism and how it had affected my relationships with others. Soon I began to see that old relationships, even those with my siblings, were different than I had thought they were. Having enthroned myself as my siblings' protective substitute mother, I had denied the normal sibling jealousies that accompany childhood. My Fourth Step writing revealed that those jealousies had not gone away, but rather had grown with us, and now involved our children, too. Not allowing myself and my siblings to be simply children had only slowed our maturing process and built walls between us.

Day by day, week by week, my vision cleared. I began to see who I really was. Often I didn't like what I found. In fact, many times I was amazed at how blinding my denial had been and how the defects I was comfortable with and willing to acknowledge had protected me from the real shameful and painful ones. Viewing myself as someone's victim had made it seem O.K. to be self-absorbed and rage-filled. Failing to accept responsibility for my actions had robbed me of spiritual growth. The more defects I saw, the harder it became to fulfill the one requirement my sponsor had insisted upon.

Even though writing my Fourth Step was not always "fearless," well organized or pleasant, I continued to plod through. I began to let my Higher Power help me, and I wrote whatever came into my mind each day. Some days I felt nauseated by the memories of how the first sex addict in my life, my father, had victimized me. Other days I was saddened by memories that came up and dismayed at what I was finding out about the real me. Even so, I continued until I felt I had uncovered every secret I had hidden deep within. At times I felt overwhelmed with shame and painful feelings, but I'm grateful to my Higher Power for giving me the courage to face the feelings and move on. I am also grateful for my sponsor's wisdom in encouraging me to find my assets. Ending each writing on a positive note helped to keep me moving forward, and I began to feel compassion for myself and others.

Some days I moved forward a page, others only a paragraph. Many days the paper was blotched with tears, but a wonderful thing happened. As the tears washed my eyes, a clearer picture of myself emerged. I was not really better or worse than other human beings. I found that I was, after all, just a person on a journey — and that has made a tremendous difference in my recovery and my life.

•   •   •

I was a member of S-Anon for several years before I completed my Fourth Step. I had started to work on it a number of times, but lacked the courage, the willingness and the foundation to complete it. I feared the changes I thought I would have to make if I did this Step. After I had really developed a trusting relationship with my Higher Power and I truly understood that Steps One, Two, and Three formed a solid foundation for me, my fear seemed to dissipate, and I finally felt ready to do the Fourth Step.

By that time I also realized that "searching and fearless" did not mean "burdensome and guilty." I was just asked to take a thorough and honest look at my attitudes and behaviors to this point. As I inventoried, I spent at least as much time looking at my assets as defects. This was important because of my tendency to discount my positive characteristics. Looking at my assets helped me realize that although I had spent many years struggling with and suffering from my reactions to sexaholism, I had also developed some qualities of which I could be proud, such as resourcefulness, courage, and empathy.

I did use some guides and books to help me think of examples, but in the end, I took an overall look at my assets and defects and made my own categories to pull them all together (for example, Control, Rage, etc.). I particularly looked for patterns of behavior and instances where one defect triggered another. For example, generally when I became afraid, I tried to control others — especially my sexaholic spouse — expecting them to rescue me. Of course, because I didn't voice these (often unrealistic) expectations, I set myself up for resentment and obsession.

I asked my Higher Power to help me overcome my sense of having to do this Step perfectly. Without the help of my Higher Power, I'd still be "working on it" today! I set a date with my sponsor to give my Fifth Step while I was still writing my inventory. This supported my work, even though I did need to extend the date several times. I also scheduled time to work on my inventory. There was always something else to do — even washing the dishes could become an urgent task when my tendency toward procrastination came up!

I can see now that I completed my Fourth Step at a time when an honest look at myself was just what was needed to move ahead and grow in my program. Steps One through Three had helped me surrender my sexaholic husband. I soon realized it was important to look at my past behavior and let go of it, so that I could continue to grow in my recovery. My Higher Power led me through the process by helping me remember the people and situations I needed to recall — and by providing the help and support of other loving S-Anons to get me through the experience.

•   •   •

Approximately two years into my S-Anon recovery I completed a very thorough Fourth Step inventory. I was working on the Steps with some other S-Anons, and we worked through examples of character defects and assets, along with questions that helped us write about particular defects or assets. I had a lot to write on each character defect — until I got to the defect of isolation. I didn't think isolation was an issue for me. In meetings I heard some people say that prior to coming to S-Anon they had cut themselves off from friends and social activities through obsessing about another person's lusting. I couldn't relate to those stories. I went to work every day, kept in contact with friends, and rarely declined invitations to social activities. I had nothing to write about isolation, so I just put a big "X" through that page and continued until I finished the inventory. Through doing my Fourth Step, I learned that I had already made a lot of progress in the program. I learned that I had many character strengths hiding under defects. Doing the inventory was a very affirming experience. It was clear I was already receiving the benefits of applying the program to my everyday life.

About three years later, I was asked to share my experience, strength, and hope on the Fourth Step at an S-Anon weekend gathering. I reviewed my old Step notes before going to the gathering so I could reflect on the experience of doing my inventory. I was astonished to discover that I had put a big "X" through the page on isolation. I was grateful that I had grown in my understanding of isolation! Through working the S-Anon program I had come to realize that isolation is not just a physical separation from people and activities. Even though I surrounded myself with people, I clearly isolated emotionally and spiritually from other people and from my Higher Power by not sharing my pain, anger or fears with anyone. While I was always available to help with the problems of others, I pretended I didn't have any problems. I believed that no one would love me as I am, including God. I never lost my belief in God, but I was disconnected from God. Connecting emotionally and spiritually with other S-Anon members helped me return to my God connection. While I was as honest as I was able to be at the time I completed my Fourth Step inventory, I was grateful that this opportunity to re-visit the Step really helped clarify that God is guiding my recovery process and that my Higher Power doesn't want me to do my recovery work alone.

PRACTICING
THESE
PRINCIPLES

℘

S tep Four suggests that we make a searching and fearless moral inventory of ourselves, yet many of us found that fear caused us to postpone this inventory. We were afraid of what we would find, afraid that shedding light on ourselves would uncover so many shortcomings that we could not bear the truth about ourselves. This Step is about an honest examination of our true nature, good and bad; a process of self-discovery guided by our Higher Power. This process can be painful at times, particularly when we see that we, not others, are often the source of many of our problems. On the other hand, it is rewarding and enlightening to see the personal strengths that our inventory reveals. Many of us have noticed with irony that a consequence of not doing this Step is generally a continuance of the very pain we originally wished to avoid.

> *Though our [Third Step] decision was a vital and crucial step, it could have little permanent effect unless at once followed by a strenuous effort to face, and to be rid of, the things in ourselves which had been blocking us. ...we had to get down to causes and conditions.*[8]

Our Fourth Step inventory also helps us develop the humility that lays a necessary foundation for our growing Twelve Step recov-

---

[8] *Alcoholics Anonymous,* p. 64.

ery. Each time we look at ourselves and our problems in the light of the Fourth Step, we put to the test the critical attitudes of honesty, open-mindedness, and willingness. For example, many of us were able to justify to ourselves a great deal of procrastination when we thought about working this Step and Step Five. In fact, some of us thought that "thinking about it" would be sufficient. We found, though, that working this Step as outlined in our literature was just what we needed when we felt stalled in our recovery or when we thought "this program isn't working for me like it works for other people." When we took the time to write out our inventories, our resentments, and our reflections on questions like the ones listed below, our self-examination began to pay off. It helped us to see and accept things we had hidden, even from ourselves. As one member put it, "Believing in the Steps gave me hope, but working them gave me the promised results."

In making the inventory, some write a history of self-defeating behaviors in past relationships, many follow the format in Chapter Five (pp. 64-71) of *Alcoholics Anonymous*, others focus on examining themselves in the context of a list of character qualities such as the one found in Al-Anon's *Blueprint for Progress* and some write an autobiography, taking care to look at motivations for past behaviors. Our sponsor or others in the program can help direct us with their experience, strength and hope. As we take inventory, we remember that thoroughness is our aim, not perfection, and we use the principles of our program as suggested in our Conference-Approved Literature, not guilty comparisons with others, as a guide.

•   •   •

STEP FOUR

Made a searching and fearless moral inventory of ourselves.

❧ Have I delayed working the Fourth Step? If so, why?

❧ What are the significant events or relationships in my life? Do I have any confusion, fear or uneasiness about them? Do they raise for me any resentment, worry, anger, self-pity, depression or a compulsion to control? What was my part (and not my part) in these troubling situations or relationships? Where did I cause harm to myself or others? Is there a behavior pattern in these events or relationships?

∞ When have my human instincts for material and emotional security, for companionship and for sex crossed the line from being a desire to becoming a demand (that is, changed from a God-given instinct to a defect of character)?

∞ Which of my attitudes or actions are keeping me from achieving serenity and being of true service to God and others? Are fear, resentment, pride or shame related to these attitudes and actions?

∞ Remembering that rigorous honesty is a cornerstone of recovery, what am I most afraid to admit to myself?

∞ What can I appreciate about my life and character? What are my assets? Which of my personal qualities have benefited myself and others? Has there been a positive aspect to any of my character defects?

∞ As I think about the work I have done on my Fourth Step, is there any part where I have focused more on another person, perhaps the sexaholic, than on myself? Is there any place where I have assigned blame? What might be my motivation? How might I apply the first three Steps to this?

∞ If I have previously worked the Fourth Step, what issue(s) might be blocking my spiritual progress now? Remembering the benefits I received in working my last Fourth Step, how can I apply Step Four to current issue(s)?

STEP FIVE

❦

*Admitted to God,
to ourselves, and
to another human being
the exact nature
of our wrongs.*

Step Four revealed to us the character defects that had been hiding under our compulsive behavior. We began to see exactly what was keeping us from the serenity we longed for. Now, Step Five contains a three-fold task: admitting to God, to ourselves, and to another human being the exact nature of our wrongs. All the Steps help us reduce our pride, but Step Five might be considered the toughest challenge yet. Many of us found it the hardest one to do, but it is the most necessary Step for our peace of mind.

We first admitted our defects to God. We weren't telling God something He didn't already know. The benefit lies in being able to see ourselves and being able to acknowledge what we see. It also helps us to learn how to communicate intimately with our Higher Power. With His help we became aware of the areas in our lives we needed to change. Admitting these things to God was also the beginning of receiving forgiveness and the ability to forgive others.

Next, Step Five asks us to admit our shortcomings to ourselves. At first, we were tempted to think the sexaholic had all the character defects in the family, but as we opened our hearts to our Higher Power we began to see we could not continue to justify our hostile feelings about ourselves and others. It is helpful to check our Step Four inventory for defects such as resentment, rage, suspicion, self-pity, and personal secrets (humiliating experiences we had not shared with anyone). We saw that even if we did not start conflicts with others, our reactions and responses contributed to the negativity and hurt us and them. It is hard to look at ourselves and admit we are often wrong.

Finally, it seems that genuine humility can not be reached without admitting our character defects to another human being. At this stage, we may struggle with some fear or embarrassment and say, "Why can't this just be taken to God? Let's leave other people out of this." There are several difficulties with this way of thinking. First, until we are willing to openly say out loud what we've been hiding for so long, our good intentions to change are merely theoretical. When we reveal our shortcomings, the person who hears them becomes witness to our decision to change. The second difficulty with confining our disclosure to God is that we may rationalize our behavior with subtle excuses. We are not capable of seeing ourselves objectively. One advantage of talking to another person is that after listening to us they may have insights and counsel. We have learned that going it alone in spiritual matters is not wise.

In choosing another person to confide in we make sure that they are experienced, living in emotional and spiritual recovery, and overcoming their own obstacles. We could choose a sponsor, another program member, a clergyman, a therapist, or someone else. Usually we do not choose the sexaholic or a family member as the person who will hear our Fifth Step.

After we decided on a person, it took great courage to begin our disclosure. As we spoke openly and honestly, we were happily surprised with how well we were received. We found that the person responded with compassionate understanding and sometimes shared their own personal stories. We felt great relief as pent-up emotions flooded out of us. Looking at ourselves in the light dispels the dark clouds. Our fear of not being loved for who we really are dissolves, and we feel genuine acceptance from others.

We derive many things from Step Five. Coming out of isolation is one benefit. Most of us came into S-Anon feeling deeply lonely. Many of us had suffered since childhood with a sense of not belonging. When we reached S-Anon we found ourselves among people who really understood, and a sense of belonging began to grow inside. But hearing others share in a way that we strongly identify with is not the only thing that makes us feel that we belong. We come to realize that we need to speak with complete honesty about our own conflicts to reach true kinship with God and others.

Another benefit of working Step Five is an increase in the character quality of humility. Humility has been defined as the accurate assessment of one's self, so the first practical move toward developing this attribute is to recognize who and what we are. Then we make a sincere attempt to become all that we can.

We emerge from isolation, and when we risk sharing our stories with supportive people, our guilt is relieved and we come to a place of greater peace:

> The dammed-up emotions of years break out of their confinement, and miraculously vanish as soon as they are exposed. As the pain subsides, a healing tranquility takes its place. And when humility and serenity are so combined, something else of a great moment is apt to occur. ... Even those who had faith already often become conscious of God as they never were before. [9]

•   •   •

---

[9] [Alcoholics Anonymous] *Twelve Steps and Twelve Traditions*, p. 62.

Step Five
STORIES

When I was about half way through my Fourth Step inventory, I made a date with my sponsor to do the sharing with "another human being" part of my Fifth Step. Since she lived in a distant city, this date coincided with the next time my husband and I were scheduled to be there for business. I continued to work on my inventory as the deadline approached.

I finally completed my Fourth Step the night before leaving to see her. I was ecstatic to have the burden lifted, at the same time I was filled with fearful obsession over what I imagined was to come. I had dared to be completely honest in my Fourth Step, writing down things I had never told another person. I was afraid of sharing certain shameful parts of the inventory with her, even though she had never given me any reason to be afraid.

On the plane ride there, I started feeling sick. At first I thought it was just the physical manifestation of my fear, but before long it became clear that I was really sick with the flu. I couldn't believe it — I had worked so hard to be ready and now this! I knew it would be months before I could see my sponsor again, and I wanted to do the Fifth Step in person, so we forged ahead.

In my weakened physical condition, I did not have the energy to do my usual routine of "putting the best face on things." Instead I bared my soul — truly for the first time. I was amazed. My sponsor accepted me just as I was, at my very worst. Her nurturing support gave me the courage to go on, particularly as the shameful items moved closer and closer to the top of my sharing list. I couldn't believe it when she didn't bat an eye at the stuff I had been so afraid to reveal. She just nodded her head in support. When I was done sharing, she suggested that some of the shame I had been walking around with was not really mine to carry. As for the rest of the defects, she smiled and said I was "a pretty average S-Anon." She also validated my strengths and even came up with some I had never considered.

I felt relieved and even proud — I had completed this part of the Fifth Step. While I do not recommend the "flu method," it certainly was a blessing to me. It shattered the remaining layer of emotional isolation that was so characteristic of me previously. More important, my willingness to finally get honest and my sponsor's acceptance was a springboard for my own self-acceptance and for my belief that my Higher Power accepts me just as I am. The experience seemed to melt my fear about opening up with God. When I did share the truth about myself with my Higher Power, I finally started to have a real relationship with God. It was a turning point in my recovery.

• • •

After all the hard work of honestly looking at my character defects, I felt relieved to move on to my Fifth Step. I had scheduled a date with my sponsor to share my discoveries about myself while I was still completing my inventory. Because of my tendency to procrastinate, setting a date was an important part of working this Step for me.

I was fortunate to have developed a good relationship with my sponsor before I began work on my Fourth and Fifth Steps. She had helped me learn how to trust appropriately again, and the sense of trust I felt with her supported me and made me feel it was safe to share my assets and defects with her. I knew ahead of time she would not judge me, but rather, be able to listen to me with love. I spoke with her regularly while I was writing my inventory. I laughed with her about my procrastination and honestly talked about my fears. Her encouragement was vital to the process.

I had a lot to share, so I did my Fifth Step in two evenings with my sponsor. I began by talking about issues that were hard for me to reveal, so that they would be out of the way. (For example, the sexual acting out I had participated in with my husband to try to control him.) I learned a lot just by reading my inventory to my sponsor. I began to see even more patterns of behavior emerge, for example, the way resentments lead me to feelings of superiority and entitlement. My sponsor was also helpful in recognizing and pointing out some new connections to me, for example, the way anger often masked my fear. I occasionally even had a chance to inject my sense of humor (one of my assets) as I saw just how persistent some of my defects really were. I'm grateful that nowhere does it say that the Fifth Step needs to be a grueling and torturous procedure!

As I completed my sharing I was overcome with relief and a great sense of accomplishment. I felt that I had truly done a searching and fearless inventory with my Higher Power's help, and now I had been granted the courage to share it honestly with my sponsor. After sharing with her, I offered my Fourth Step in prayer to my Higher Power. Soon after, I shared my Fourth and Fifth Step experience at a meeting. This, too, was an accomplishment. After several years of attending meetings and many frustrating attempts, I had "worked the program" through Step Five! I felt able to put the past behind me and move on.

●   ●   ●

I know that many of us come into S-Anon feeling deeply lonely with a strong sense of not belonging. I definitely felt that when I came in. This loneliness and isolation made the prospect of admitting my wrongs to God and to another human being very hard. Underneath, though, I knew the Fifth Step would bring me freedom and peace. So using the principle of this Step, I chose to admit my worst secret to my group and to God — that I had stood by and done nothing about my daughter's incest. It was very painful to admit that I had not been there for her and that I had not been the mother she needed — that I had been so out of touch with my reality and hers. As I had hoped, admitting it to the group brought me a sense of forgiveness and healing. Some of the group members were the age of my children. Feeling their compassion and forgiveness was particularly healing for me. One even came up to me and said she wished that I was her mom, because I was able to admit my wrongs and say that I was sorry.

After doing the Fifth Step on this issue I gradually forgave myself and released the guilt. My life is now increasingly better on a daily basis, even though I still occasionally feel some sadness when I think of how my actions affected my children. Yet I am grateful that I was able to share the secret. Sharing it gave me the strength that comes with knowing I can identify my truths and I can share them. Sharing about my denial of the incest also gave me the courage to go on and formally work an entire Fifth Step with my sponsor. Today when I'm stuck in difficult feelings or a problem, I turn to Step Five. It helps me live in reality.

• • •

PRACTICING
THESE
PRINCIPLES

༭

In Step Five we share our Fourth Step with another person and with God. We admit our findings to them and to ourselves and also discuss the causes for our attitudes and behavior. Many of us had not made a practice of being totally honest and were terrified at the prospect. We had secrets, some shameful, and we feared bringing them into the light. We thought to ourselves, "Isn't it enough that I did the Fourth Step? Why do I have to share these things?"

Surprisingly, we discovered that sharing them with our Higher Power and someone else was one of the most freeing things we had ever experienced. Most found that

> *We are only as sick as our secrets. Step Five does not ask us to show our faults to the whole world, but to our own hearts, to the God of our understanding and to a trusted friend.*[10]

doing this Step was a turning point in recovery as we took the principles of humility and honesty, which underlie all the Steps, and put them into practice. Our good intentions to work the Steps became concrete actions. Forgiveness and acceptance from another person spurred the beginning of these qualities in ourselves. We felt better able to communicate with others and with our Higher Power. We

---

[10] *Paths to Recovery: Al-Anon's Steps, Traditions and Concepts*, p. 53.

began to learn how to really trust and how to let go of the shame and secrets that had held us back. We had a new-found ability to be progressively more honest in all areas of our life. We found healing, peace of mind and serenity.

Many of us choose to work our Fifth Step with our sponsor, but any person who understands our purpose in sharing and can keep a confidence can do this service (for example, a therapist, doctor, or member of the clergy). We generally find it is not helpful to do the Fifth Step with the sexaholic, a family member or anyone who may be adversely affected by hearing it or who does not understand the Twelve Steps.

In sharing, we are honest and make a particular point of sharing those things we feel reluctant to discuss. In listening to another's response to our Step, we try to keep an open mind. We trust that our Higher Power is guiding the process. Finally, after working the Fifth Step, many make a practice of observing a brief time of quiet reflection and closure as suggested on page 75 of *Alcoholics Anonymous*.

•   •   •

STEP FIVE

Admitted to God, to ourselves, and to another human being the exact nature of our wrongs.

∞ Do I regularly share myself — my feelings, thoughts, problems — with my Higher Power and others? Or do I tend toward extreme self-reliance, waiting to share until after I have either worked out the situation or exploded in rage (unfortunately often keeping myself in the problem)? How might the Step Five process of opening up and sharing with another person change the way I look at myself?

❧ What fears do I have about the Fifth Step? Have I delayed doing the Fifth Step? If so, why?

❧ Having completed Step Four, what is "the exact nature of my wrongs?" What are those things I really do not want to admit? What do I want to hide from others? What might be keeping me from admitting these things?

❧ What assets do I have to share? Do I have a hard time acknowledging good things about myself? How might the Fifth Step help me with this?

❧ How can I work my Fifth Step with my Higher Power? Who are people who could serve as a listener for my Fifth Step? Do I feel comfortable discussing specifics like location, ground rules, etc. ahead of time with the person who will hear my Fifth Step?

❧ As I reflect on having done my Fifth Step, what did I gain? How did it affect my recovery? What, if anything, would I do differently if I have cause to come back to Step Five?

❧ Considering my work in the first five Steps, is there anything that feels unresolved — a nagging issue I might revisit or rework through these Steps?

❧ If I have done Step Five previously, how can I continue to use Step Five in connection with my Tenth Step inventories?

STEP SIX

⚭

*Were entirely ready
to have God
remove all these defects
of character.*

Steps Four and Five lead us to uncover our character defects. We face them, write them out, and share them with another person without self-condemnation. In Step Six we become entirely ready to have God remove these defects. This is not to imply that we must become perfectly ready, but we must be willing and open-minded. It is this state of willingness that we seek in Step Six. We become willing to have our defects removed, not just lessened or made milder. Like our compulsive thinking, our defects grow progressively worse with time. It is useless to think of clinging to a defect and trying to keep it "in check."

We are not powerful enough to remove our defects of character, but we have come to believe in a Power greater than ourselves, and we are willing to have our Higher Power remove our defects. All we do is present ourselves to our Higher Power with a willing heart.

Can or will God remove these defects of character? The answer is an affirming YES! God has done this for many people in Twelve Step recovery all over the world, but God always respects our free will. Nothing can be done until we are "entirely ready."

We worked against ourselves in many detrimental ways in the past. First, we tried to remove the character defects of the sexaholic. Then, we tried to remove our own hurt and rage, but our attempts were futile. We begin to realize that only a Higher Power can do the job. God will certainly remove our defects and shortcomings if we ask Him.

In the past our understanding of such words as giving, helping, and loving had become confused. We gave, helped and loved others only in an effort to change or manipulate them. Our love was conditional; we expected a return on our investment. In turn, we blamed others for not giving us what we expected. Our ulterior motives for loving were hidden, even from ourselves. We did not know how to express our own feelings and needs to others. We did not know how to be responsible for our own happiness. We tried to use the sexaholic to make us happy instead of developing our understanding of God's presence within us.

Becoming "entirely ready to have God remove all these defects of character" is one of the most beneficial processes we will go through in our lifetime. But it doesn't mean all our defects will be lifted out instantly. Some might go right away. Others will go in time. Still other defects will improve with patient adherence to the principles of our program. We always want to aim for the best, even though we know that we cannot be perfect. We accept ourselves, as we travel at our own pace towards spiritual growth.

In the same way that no one is perfect, no one is ever "entirely ready." All we can do is try, but that is a vast improvement over saying "I will never give up these defects." Maybe we said that in another way, such as, "I know I'm right." Short of refusing to give them up, most of us have to admit that we have loved our defects. They were our defenses against the world, and they served us well from time to time. After all, weren't some of our manipulations the only methods we knew to get what we wanted? It takes a brave person to step unarmed into the arena of the unknown, desiring only to relate to God and others with honesty and intimacy for the first time. We must admit the old ways haven't worked very well. We are now ready to let them go. We can look for reassurance to this Al-Anon wisdom, "… God does not remove a fault to produce a vacuum, but to make room for one of His ideas: love, kindness, tolerance."[11]

---

[11] *The Dilemma of the Alcoholic Marriage*, p. 85.

If we find that we still have trouble letting go of our character defects, we can ask God to help us to be willing. Remember, willingness is the key to Step Six.

•   •   •

Like so many in S-Anon who struggle with perfectionism, I initially experienced the words "entirely ready" as a huge obstacle. I thought I needed to achieve a state of perfect readiness in order to have my defects removed. I thought I could make Step Six "happen" if I somehow worked the perfect program.

Step Six STORIES

Working the S-Anon Steps with my sponsor has given me a new understanding of "entirely ready." I do not need to work my program perfectly and I cannot force Step Six to happen by my own doing. For me "entirely ready" now means I need only let God point out my defects that need work and then allow God to help me explore a deeper level of self-honesty. For example, within a recent two-week period I became intensely aware of my character defect of dwelling in fantasy, a refusal to accept reality by clinging to the way I think things should be and ignoring the way things are. One day I complained incessantly about the weather — "Spring shouldn't be this cold!" Another day I felt my blood pressure rise as I argued with my health insurer over the phone — "It shouldn't take two weeks to get an authorization!" Yet another day I inwardly whined about my sexaholic spouse — "Why can't he express his love for me more spontaneously?" Even as those words formed in my head, it was as if my Higher Power also gave me an awareness of just how often I was disrupting my day and my serenity by living in "the world should be my way" fantasy. Having come to a place in recovery where I trusted God and valued my serenity, I was finally ready to have God remove this roadblock from my life.

I am relieved to find that I do have a choice about the character defects that stand in the way of serenity. I need only be honest, open-minded and willing to let God bring issues to the surface as God sees that I am ready to deal with them. Today I am grateful I do not have to *make* Step Six "happen." I can just *let* it happen by keeping my mind and heart open to my Higher Power.

•　　•　　•

Like many others, a crisis brought me to S-Anon. While on a camping trip with friends, my husband was arrested for trying to expose himself to a child. I felt confused, in a lot of pain — and totally focused on him and this crisis to the exclusion of everything else in my life. My mind constantly raced: How could he do this to me? I loved him so much, and I treated him so well. Why did he have to be like this? Why couldn't God just fix him?

When I began to work the program, S-Anon members suggested that I apply the tools of the S-Anon program like the literature, slogans and writing about my problems on a daily basis. As I used them, I began to experience some serenity. Yet when the Steps were read at meetings, I noticed that the words of Step Six — that God could remove defects of character — still seemed hollow and empty. If this was true, why hadn't God removed the obvious defect in my husband's character — his sexaholism?

Despite these uncomfortable feelings, I continued to work the program. I got a sponsor and finally started to really work the Steps and practice the principles of the program. Through working Steps Four and Five I learned that I, too, had defects that stood in my way and needed to be removed. The most obvious defect was the way I focused on my husband rather than on myself — a defect that had been so evident in my reaction to the crisis that brought me to S-Anon. My pattern of focusing on my husband and his problems had been my way of denying my own problems and difficult feelings. Unfortunately, this behavior kept me in a lot of pain.

Working the Fourth and Fifth Steps helped me see just how

much this "outward" focusing had hurt me. I realized that when I focused on my husband I was not able to focus on God's plan for me. That was when I finally became willing to surrender this character defect to God. Today I am continuing to practice Step Six by remaining open each day to any revelations God has for me about my shortcomings. I am finding serenity and happiness in my life and my marriage by learning to focus on myself and by allowing my Higher Power to help me.

• • •

By working Steps Four and Five I became aware that jealousy had always been a major problem for me. Even though my recovering partner and I had not yet made a formal commitment to each other, I resented any woman with whom he interacted, regardless of whether or not there was cause to be angry. My resentful feelings were especially acute when my fear of rejection and abandonment surfaced. I acted out these feelings by pouting and withdrawing from my partner and being cold and distant toward the woman. When anger fueled my jealousy, it really did seem that I could control my partner with the force of my angry feelings. I had difficulty understanding that what I had used to survive in this relationship was a "character defect." I could not imagine how our relationship would last if I was not trying to control how he related to other women.

I talked about my jealousy character defect in my Fifth Step, and from time to time I did feel willing to have the jealousy removed, but my fear was great, and I did not know how to become any more "ready." I tried replacing feelings of inadequacy and inferiority with thoughts of the love and care of my Higher Power. I knew I needed to get my sense of self-worth from a relationship with a real Higher Power, not a human one, but I still struggled with being "entirely ready."

One night I sat outside his apartment in my car, knowing that a woman with whom he had been in treatment was visiting him. He was working a good recovery program and I was seeing the results of that, so I had no reason to believe there was anything inappropriate about her visit with him. Yet my jealousy, driven by feelings of betrayal from the past, made my pain nearly unbearable. I hated my partner, the woman, and myself, and I felt like a rat in a trap with no way out. I knew I could never be happy, joyous and free if I was jealous of every woman with whom he had a conversation. I thought to myself, "I can't live this way," and for the first time I finally accepted the truth that my partner's attention was his to give, not mine to control. God granted me a gut-level awareness that the pain of holding onto my jealousy was worse than the pain would be if the relationship ended (my greatest fear). In that moment I finally felt entirely ready to be rid of my jealousy.

This process of becoming entirely ready was a powerful lesson in how a particular defect works for me (for example, by providing an illusion of control) and works against me (usually by reducing my ability to love and care for others and myself). I learned that becoming "willing" takes as long as it takes. The pain of holding onto this destructive defect of character had to become worse than my fear of change. This incident helped me learn that regardless of the issue, I can turn my will and my life as well as my character defects over to my Higher Power, trusting in His love and care for me.

•   •   •

PRACTICING
THESE
PRINCIPLES

☙

How could we ever become entirely ready to have God remove all our defects of character? Many of us confused *entirely* ready with *perfectly* ready. We did not understand that Step Six is not an action Step on our part. Rather, Step Six is about adopting an attitude of open-mindedness and willingness to finally see our defects as the hindrances they are. Whether the character shortcoming is control, resentment, fear, excessive need to take care of others, a need to blame others, or countless other obstacles to serenity, our Higher Power can remove the defect if we are willing to let go.

We recall from our Step Four experience that having defects of character does not mean we are defective or bad,

Only Step One, where we made the 100 percent admission we were powerless ... can be practiced with absolute perfection. The remaining eleven Steps state perfect ideals. They are goals toward which we look, and the measuring sticks by which we estimate our progress. Seen in this light, Step Six is still difficult, but not at all impossible. The only urgent thing is that we make a beginning, and keep trying.[12]

---

[12] [Alcoholics Anonymous] *Twelve Steps and Twelve Traditions*, p. 68.

but simply that we are human beings in need of assistance from a Higher Power. Now we trust that God guides our Step Six process, bringing to our awareness those defects that impede our growth. We begin to notice the defects, seeing them for what they are. Then we finally become willing to surrender them to our Higher Power. This noticing and willingness is all Step Six requires.

If we are unwilling or fearful, we can begin by asking God to start with those defects and replace them with the willingness, courage, and trust to proceed. If we find that situations in our lives seem to get worse as we work Step Six, we relax and remind ourselves that God is simply bringing our defects to the surface. As we grow in our understanding of these spiritual principles, we thank our Higher Power for our defects, which continually remind us of our humanity and the need for God in our lives. We finally understand "Thy will, not mine, be done."

•   •   •

STEP SIX

Were entirely ready to have God remove
all these defects of character.

❧ What have I learned from the experiences of other S-Anons, such as my sponsor, about becoming entirely ready to have a Higher Power remove defects of character?

❧ What does "entirely ready" mean to me? When will I know I am entirely ready? Is there anything standing in the way of my being entirely ready to have God remove all my defects of character? How can my Higher Power help me with this?

෨ What are my defects of character as uncovered in my Fourth Step inventory? What are workable and helpful characteristics with which God can replace my defects?

෨ In addition to these defects, what other things may hinder my serenity and stand in the way of my usefulness to God and others (for example, old coping strategies, old attitudes, feelings I am stuck in or other self-created obstacles)?

෨ Regarding the defect that is currently most problematic for me, what purpose does the defect serve? How does it seem to be helping me? What price am I paying for holding on to this defect?

෨ Have I tried to remove my own character defects by working a better program, trying not to let them show or otherwise relying on myself and my own actions? Am I ready to develop an attitude of willingness to surrender these defects to my Higher Power? What are some tools I can use to become willing?

෨ Is there any area of my life where I still depend only on myself or believe that will power is the answer? If so, how can my Higher Power help?

෨ What can I be grateful for in my life?

STEP SEVEN

❧

Humbly asked Him to remove our shortcomings.

We frequently misunderstand the word humility. Often we think it implies weakness, lack of character, or helplessness. In a world that exalts fame and fortune, humility does not seem like a desirable quality. Instead, we believe success requires pride and ambition.

Many of us spent years achieving the kind of success we could measure in money and material possessions. We tried to be successful in our careers and thought that was a way to guarantee happiness. We acquired comfortable homes and thought that would guarantee comfort. We thought we could guarantee a secure future through hard work and intelligence. We thought meeting our physical and material needs were the primary goals of our lives. We were not necessarily wrong. It's just that we left out some important priorities.

Even though we meant well, we hindered ourselves with our lack of humility. We didn't realize how important humility is in building our characters. Nor did we see that spiritual needs have to come before any others. At times we did have a sincere desire to build our characters, but when we had to choose between character and comfort, somehow comfort always won.

In S-Anon we learned that pride and fear were the motives for much of our irrational behavior. We feared we would never get the things our pride told us we deserved. We feared we would lose the relationships and material possessions we had. We lived in a constant state of turmoil and restlessness. We had to find a way to reduce our unreasonable expectations and find peace.

In Step Seven we find a way to settle our emotional turmoil and make a move toward God. Only God could remove our obsession with the sexaholic, and only God can remove our defects of character. As we approach Step Seven, most of us have learned to call upon God in times of great need. We really have begun to desire humility, instead of just accepting it as something we "should" want. We have learned we can accomplish more with a humble attitude than we can when we are prideful and fearful. Humility works better not only when we are asking God for help, but also when we are dealing with the people in our lives. Humility allows us to ask for and accept God's forgiveness. With that forgiveness, our consciences can be at ease. As long as we place genuine reliance upon a Higher Power, our humility is at work. If we return to relying on our own strength and intelligence, we are still trying to play God.

Step Seven requires faith, as do so many of these Steps. Just as we came to believe in Step Two that a "Power greater than ourselves could restore us to sanity," so do we come to believe in Step Seven that God can remove our shortcomings. We have to believe before it can happen.

It has been difficult to take steps of faith and to develop a more hopeful perspective on life. In fact, it is often painful. Most of us have spent much of our lives running from pain. We seldom wanted to accept suffering or accept the idea that suffering could help us develop character and humility. Now we are beginning to fear pain less. We see that pain paves the road to many new realizations about ourselves, others and God. Listening to people in S-Anon, we grasp the reality that despair and failure can be transformed into hope and success.

Since we have taken an honest look at character defects, discussed them with another person and become willing to have them removed, we have begun to experience some peace. As we now ask God to remove our shortcomings, even more tranquility will come to us. We can enjoy true peace for longer periods of time.

Some of us also notice an improvement in our attitude toward God. Some of us came to S-Anon with no belief in a Higher Power.

Others of us believed, but were angry at God for not preventing sex-aholism from invading our lives. Others were just plain confused. By the time we are ready and willing to take Step Seven, we have built some trust in our Higher Power, and we are developing a spiritual life and a relationship with God as we understand Him. We might approach this Step in a way similar to the following prayer:

> My Creator, I am now willing that you should have all of me, good and bad. I pray that you now remove from me every single defect of character which stands in the way of my usefulness to you and my fellows. Grant me strength, as I go out from here, to do your bidding. Amen.[13]

Of course, that is only a suggestion. Your own words can beautifully express much of the same feeling. The important thing is that we humbly ask God to remove our shortcomings.

•   •   •

After I got over the shock and disbelief of learning about my spouse's betrayal, all I could feel was hurt and anger. Reminders of his cheating were everywhere and they sparked feelings of humiliation and shame. I wanted revenge for my hurt pride, so I berated and belittled my husband. While my vengeful behavior brought fleeting satisfaction, it never brought joy or happiness. I thought about  leaving, but I realized that wouldn't take away the pain. I still felt love for him. Despite these realizations, I felt entitled to my anger, but the price I had to pay for clinging to that anger was more pain.

---

[13] *Alcoholics Anonymous*, p. 76

As I worked the S-Anon program, it became clear to me that while I had a legitimate reason for feeling offended, I would not stop hurting until I made a decision to let it go. Why did I let resentment, hurt, and fear torment me for so long? Hadn't I suffered enough? I could not forgive. I was afraid that forgiving would mean pretending the betrayal didn't happen or denying my need to take some space and time to establish trust and intimacy again. But to forgive didn't mean those things. It only meant that I had to choose to give up my preoccupation with revenge, berating and belittling. I had to make a decision to surrender my self-righteous desire to hang onto the offended feelings.

So I decided to let them go. I knew I couldn't get rid of the bitterness and anger by myself. I had to have God's help. I got that help using the Seventh Step prayer found on page 76 of *Alcoholics Anonymous*. I surrendered, humbly asking God to remove my bitterness and anger over what my husband had done and to return the loving feelings for my husband I had felt previously. The gift I got was freedom from the pain associated with the wrongs. I was given the gift of peace.

Just as I asked in my heart specifically that the defect of ongoing bitterness and anger be removed, today I adapt this prayer to every problem that "stands in the way of my usefulness to God and my fellows." It has always worked if I really wanted to be free of a defect. Surrendering through Step Seven always brings me a sense of joy and release.

•   •   •

I was afraid that if I asked God to remove my shortcomings, I would have nothing left. I was particularly fearful about short-comings I had gotten a lot of mileage out of —- sarcasm, arguing with my spouse, being resentful over his acting-out with men, etc. What would I do with all the time I spent thinking about the other person, the time I spent obsessing about the "problem," the time I spent telling people how unfair it was? Indeed, that time could be better spent in countless other ways, but letting go of shortcomings can be difficult. S-Anon helped me find the clarity to ask myself, "Is this defect really so useful — particularly when it also brings up the hurt, humiliation and guilt of my past?" Even though my answer is usually "No," I sometimes still hesitate to ask God to remove my shortcomings.

I remember one incident very clearly. I was in a restaurant observing (actually judging) people around me. I was consumed with thoughts of how people should order, should look, should dress, should, should and more should. I was so preoccupied with "correcting" all these people that I lost sight of the reason I was at the restaurant — to enjoy myself and my dinner companions! Feeling my serenity disrupted, I momentarily stopped myself and thought about what was happening. I became aware that being judgmental of others was a real problem in my daily life and that this lack of humility prevented me from enjoying my own life and appreciating others as God created them. I tried to think of good things about the people in the restaurant but quickly again fell into self-righteous "correcting" instead of concentrating on what was in front of me. Finally, I remembered Step Seven and silently said, "God, please take these thoughts." Amazingly, relief was just a prayer away! God removed the obsessive, judgmental thoughts, and I finally focused on enjoying my dinner companions.

Sometimes it feels as if I am on an island surrounded by my defects of character and I will never be rid of them all. Then I remember that Step Seven tells me I am not able personally to elim-inate my shortcomings. All I need is willingness to have them removed and a humble heart to ask the God of my understanding to release me from the self-defeating shortcomings from which I want to be free.

• • •

A recent work situation gave me an opportunity to apply Step Seven. My Higher Power provided me with insight into how the relationships between my co-worker, my boss and me were similar to the relationships I had growing up in my family of origin. My part in the workplace triangle became clear to me. I saw just how willing I was to compete against my co-workers to win acceptance, approval and even praise from my boss — just like I used to compete against my sister to gain approval from my mom. When I saw my role in this way, I realized I had been trapped for many years in a pattern of behavior that left me feeling helpless, victimized and alone. I knew I didn't want to compete for approval and praise any more. In prayer I asked, "God, please free me from this compulsion to compete, which has held me captive for forty years, and give me a new way of responding." That is exactly what happened. I experienced a feeling of freedom I had never felt before. The next morning I followed up by asking God to keep resentments from building up in my heart. He has, and I still feel free. I no longer feel the old need to compete for approval and praise.

It was very clear to me at the time that this particular character defect needed to be removed. Other times I don't have that clarity, but through working the Steps I have come to a place of willingness where I try to notice the shortcomings in myself that separate me from God and others. When I am holding tightly to some character defect (I can usually tell by my level of stubbornness), I ask myself these questions: What purpose does this defect serve? What is it doing for me? What price am I paying for holding onto this defect?

Then I work the Steps on the character defect. With Steps One and Two I admit that I am powerless over the character defect and that only God can restore peace to my life. With Steps Three and Four I turn my will over to God and then objectively look at the real consequences of this defect. I work Step Five by talking about the shortcoming with my sponsor and with God in prayer. Then, with the humility that accompanies the understanding that I cannot remove this defect myself, I "let go and let God" by working Step

Seven. If I still feel caught in the character defect's grasp, maybe my Higher Power has more for me to learn. I ask God to remove whatever is blocking me from becoming entirely ready to have the defect removed and then I repeat the process. I have learned that if I am willing, my Higher Power will remove the shortcoming as I am ready to let it go.

• • •

PRACTICING
THESE
PRINCIPLES

⚭

As we approached Step Seven, many of us feared that removal of our shortcomings meant God would take everything that made us who we were and leave nothing of our personality in place. Then we listened to the Step Seven successes of others. We saw that God does not take everything, but simply removes the defects that block us from truly being useful to our Higher Power and others. In Step Seven we come to view our Higher Power as a support and guide in our on-going spiritual awakening, a helper in our refining process. We ask this Power greater than ourselves to remove our shortcomings. In doing so we are relieved of the burdens of our overly self-reliant past and our unmanageable circumstances. We are freed to learn better ways of thinking and acting.

We have little choice but to accept ourselves as we are, with all our limitations. And chief among those limitations is the fact that we cannot cure ourselves. By accepting that God can do for us what we cannot do for ourselves, we begin to achieve the humility that is necessary for change to take place. In Step Seven, we put that acceptance to work. We take action. [14]

---

[14] *How Al-Anon Works for Families & Friends of Alcoholics*, p. 57.

We come to see that the foundation of Step Seven is humility, that is, a willingness to accept ourselves as we are and to accept God's help. Humility is not about weakness, submissiveness, or humiliation. Rather it is about surrendering the attitude that seems to be the root of many of our troubles: "I know best." Being humble does not mean we stop trying to take positive action on our own behalf. Instead we stop relying exclusively on our own strength and intelligence and come to genuinely trust in our Higher Power's will for us, asking God to do for us what we cannot do for ourselves.

Like Step Three, Step Seven is an action Step in the form of a prayer. For most of us, exactly how we ask God to remove our defects does not seem to matter, so long as we express our complete willingness to be changed and believe that our Higher Power can and will help us. Many take Step Seven through praying as it is traditionally understood, for example, using the Seventh Step prayer found on page 76 of *Alcoholics Anonymous*. Others request God to remove their shortcomings through methods like writing, creatively visualizing or meditating. We keep in mind that Step Seven is not about begging, pleading or groveling. Neither is it coming to our Higher Power with a wish list of exactly what we think we need. Rather, Step Seven is a process of humbly acknowledging our ongoing need to rely on God.

•　　•　　•

STEP SEVEN

Humbly asked Him to remove our shortcomings.

❧ What are my fears about working Step Seven? Am I afraid that having defects removed will leave a void in me? How can I move past my fears in working this Step?

❧ How has my Higher Power already worked in my life? What can I learn from this?

❧ How do I understand "humbly asked Him?" Is there anything about my understanding of "humbly" that is holding me back? How can I become teachable?

❧ What is my role in this Step? What is my Higher Power's role? How does the slogan "Let go and let God" apply to this Step?

❧ As I reflect on my Sixth Step, what shortcomings can I bring to my Higher Power? What are some positive characteristics with which God might replace the defects? (For example, perhaps "identifying with others" could replace "judging others.") What are some specific ways I can be willing to practice these positive traits?

❧ What words or means of communication can I use to ask God to remove my shortcomings? Have I asked my sponsor or other program members about their experience with this Step?

❧ As I surrender my defects to God, what other shortcomings are coming to the forefront for me? Am I ready to have them removed?

❧ As I have worked this Step, have I kept a balanced view of myself and my character, understanding that making mistakes and experiencing the mistakes of others is a part of the human condition? Is it O.K. for me to make mistakes?

❧ How has my Higher Power's action in my life through Step Seven changed me?

STEP EIGHT

❧

Made a list of all
persons we had harmed,
and became willing
to make amends
to them all.

Steps Eight and Nine help to heal our personal relationships. We found that in order to go on with our spiritual journey we had to look back to the wreckage we had left behind and be accountable to the people affected by it. We began this process in Step Four, when we made our moral inventory. Now we focus on the people we have hurt and the ways in which we have hurt them.

At first we may think, "Let the past stay the past. What good will it do to reopen old wounds?" Many of us were too accustomed to thinking of ourselves as the wronged party to see how we wronged others. Now we are learning that being a victim was often a choice we made and that we have other options. Our own obsessions and fears prevented us from seeing those options. The time has come now to "own" our character defects and take responsibility for the choices we made. Continuing to blame others just prolongs our misery.

As we accepted responsibility for ourselves, we began to see that some of our most "noble" qualities just perpetuated our illness. For example, we had to reconsider our overprotectiveness toward the sexaholic, our efforts to convince the sexaholic to think like we did and even our sympathy and tolerance for the sexaholic. In some cases, that sympathy allowed us to violate our own human dignity, and we transgressed against ourselves.

We chose not to say "No" when it was necessary. For example, some of us didn't say "No" to sex even when we knew it was inappropriate or unsafe. We felt we had no choice in the matter. We grew confused, blaming ourselves for the sexaholic's behavior and blaming the sexaholic for our behavior. We did not take responsibility for ourselves.

Some of us were so preoccupied with the sexaholic we neglected our children, depriving them of spiritual and emotional attention — even physical attention, at times. We took out our rage on our children, yelling at them because of our misery inside.

How many times did we ignore our friends when we got into a romantic relationship? Did we neglect our relationships in an effort to be with the sexaholic instead? Did we decline invitations to be with friends, choosing instead to wait for the sexaholic to return or to call? Did we cancel plans at the last minute to be available for the sexaholic?

Did we make the sexaholic our Higher Power, focusing on his or her needs rather than thinking "Thy will be done?" Were our minds and hearts focused on the sexaholic rather than on God?

Were we jealous of people (for example, family members or friends) who were close to the sexaholic? Did we compete with them in an effort to be the only object of the sexaholic's affection? Did we have anger and resentment at the sexaholic's parents for the way they raised him or her in an addictive home?

Was our behavior toward the sexaholic really above reproach, or do we have some amends to make for rage-filled attitudes, words or behavior? Were we spiteful? Did we want to punish him or her for all the hurt we felt? Did we want them to suffer, too? Were we condescending, shaming or blaming?

Finally, how did we treat ourselves? Most of us had to make amends for being too hard on ourselves, especially in the beginning of recovery. We saw how often the "shoulds" and "oughts" entered our vocabulary. We began to forgive ourselves, too.

We need to write down names of specific people and how we harmed them. It does not matter if those people also harmed us. We have to look at our own feelings and actions. Were we loving and forgiving or were we bitter and resentful? When we truly examined ourselves, we had to admit to a certain percentage of ill will.

We limited ourselves to listing only those people we had harmed, forgiving those who had harmed us. If we do not feel willing or able to do this, we ask our Higher Power for help until we do feel willing. Our Higher Power can bring subconscious memories to the surface if we ask Him to do so.

•   •   •

Working the first seven Steps made it very clear to me how I had harmed others through my reactions to sexaholism. Working those Steps also had helped me to become willing to follow wherever my Higher

Step Eight
STORIES

Power led me. As I began to make my Step Eight amends list, the awareness of incidents in which I had harmed others came to mind readily. I trusted that once I made the list, God would show me how to make appropriate amends.

I immediately put my children on that list. I felt great remorse about the poor relationship I had with them when they were growing up. I came to understand and accept that because I had obsessively focused on the sexaholic in our home, I had been unable to give my children the loving attention they deserved. In my frustration, I was exhausted and short-tempered with them. I yelled at them and generally made life miserable for them. To my great regret, I also forced them to listen to me criticize their father's imperfections. I needed to own up to the effect my attitude and behavior had on them. Clearly, they belonged on my amends list.

I realized that my husband also belonged on the list. I had felt betrayed and angry about how his extra-marital affairs had taken him away from my life and our home life with our children. While those feelings were natural responses to the situation, I did not deal with those feelings very well at the time and my anger turned into chronic resentment. My attitude for years was "How dare he do this to our family and me!" Consequently, I said many unkind, hurtful words to and about my spouse over the years. I needed to make amends for that harm.

My sponsor helped me understand why I needed to be on my amends list, too. She pointed out that I had been my own worst critic. I had often accepted blame and said "I'm sorry" whether I was responsible for a situation or not. She reminded me how I had put my interests and priorities, such as finishing my college degree, on the back burner time after time. I indeed had harmed myself, and I wrote my name down, too.

God brought to my mind the many others who rounded out my amends list: extended family, co-workers, people I had known socially and at church, even some who had died. Today, even though I've moved on in my Step work, I still make it a practice to review my Eighth Step list periodically and prayerfully consider if there are more things I need to be willing to do in each case. With my mind and heart in a willing place, it's amazing how my Higher Power leads me.

•   •   •

Learning about my husband's sexaholism was like living my worst nightmare. He had acted out indiscriminately with men and women — even with a family member. In my devastation and fear, I turned to a close friend I had known since kindergarten and bared my soul to her. A week later I learned that my friend had told a group of our mutual friends what I had shared in confidence. I reacted in anger, cutting off all communication with her. While she made several attempts to talk this over with me, I refused. I believed she deserved my cold treatment. I thought what she had done was unforgivable.

Then I came to S-Anon. I worked the program and saw the harm I had caused through my own reactions to sexaholism. When I got to the part of Step Eight about becoming willing to make amends, I hit a roadblock. I remembered how I had treated my friend coldly and how I had not been willing even to talk with her about the situation. Deep down I knew I needed to make amends to her for my behavior, yet I could not get past my hurt and resentment over what she had done. My sponsor referred me to the Alcoholic Anonymous "Big Book" for "the treatment" for resentment:

> This was our course: We realized that the people who wronged us were perhaps spiritually sick. Though we did not like their symptoms and the way these disturbed us, they, like ourselves, were sick too. We asked God to help us show them the same tolerance, pity, and patience that we would cheerfully grant a sick friend. When a person offended we said to ourselves, "This is a sick man. How can I be helpful to him? God save me from being angry. Thy will be done.[15]

After earnestly applying "the treatment," I still felt bitter and was not willing to make amends to my friend. Again, my sponsor directed me to the "Big Book," this time to page 552, a suggestion for release from deep-rooted resentments:

> If you have a resentment you want to be free of, if you will pray for the person or the thing that you resent, you will be free. If you will ask in prayer for everything you want for yourself to be given to them, you will be free. Ask for their health, their prosperity, their happiness, and you will be free. Even when you don't really want it for them, and your prayers are only words and you don't mean it, go ahead and do it anyway. Do it every day for two weeks and you will find you have come to mean it and to want it for them, and you will realize that where you used to feel bitterness and resentment and hatred, you now feel compassionate understanding and love.[16]

---

[15] *Alcoholics Anonymous*, p. 66-67.
[16] *Alcoholics Anonymous*, p. 552.

Following my sponsor's suggestions helped me complete the full Step Eight process — making the list and becoming *willing* to make amends to them all. While I did not condone or approve of my friend's actions, I accepted that no one could change the past. I could let it continue to hurt me or I could choose to let it go. So while I still did not *feel* forgiving, I prayed for the ability to let go of the bitter feelings and for the willingness to make amends to her. I found that taking the action of praying for her finally gave me enough freedom from the grip of resentment. I became willing to own my part and to make amends for my wrongs toward her. This experience, while at times painful and frustrating, was an important lesson in willingness. Working this full Step Eight process has brought results every time I have made the effort to try it.

•   •   •

When I came to S-Anon, I had been stuck on Step Eight in another Twelve Step program for a long time. I had a list and I knew the people to whom I needed to make amends. I was willing enough to say "I'm sorry" and to reach out to re-establish relationships with those I had harmed the most — my children from my first marriage from whom I had been estranged. Yet a thought kept going through my mind: "There's something else I have to do. There's more to this Step than I have been able to face."

Through working the Steps again from an S-Anon point of view, I experienced many changes in my life. I became aware of the nature of my own unhealthy behavior in certain relationships and situations. I experienced a wonderful freedom from feelings of guilt and shame. Then I received a letter from my sixteen-year-old daughter that felt like a slap in the face. She essentially said that she needed a mother who would take an active role in her life and that if I wanted a relationship with her, I would have to do my part by at least living in the same city as she did, rather than on another continent. Her message reminded me of a line from the "Big Book" of Alcoholics Anonymous: "The spiritual life is not a theory. We have to live it."[17]

I finally saw why it had taken me so long to become willing to really complete Step Eight — being willing to make these amends was going to mean that my life situation might have to change and that I might lose my relationship with my sexaholic partner. This was a terrifying prospect. Through my S-Anon work I had come to identify my relationship with him as being like a drug for me. I had always put the relationship ahead of everything else in my life including my children. Now I saw I had to be willing to let it go if I wanted a relationship with my daughter.

I prayed a lot after receiving the letter, asking my Higher Power for knowledge of His will for me and the power to carry that out. The answer gradually became clear that my spiritual program would not move forward if I was not willing to actively make these amends by picking up and moving to where my children lived. I needed to make myself available for whatever relationship my Higher Power would establish between my children and me. Finally, five years after I first heard Step Eight read, God led me to place my spiritual growth as a higher priority than maintaining my primary relationship, even though I loved my partner dearly. I was really willing to leave him if I had to, for whatever time it would take. Then the miracles began to happen!

My partner and I agreed (after years of postponing the decision) to marry as soon as we could. We made plans to leave the city where we had met and lived for many years, trusting that we were in the care of a Power greater than ourselves. We have never regretted it. I reconnected in a meaningful way with my children and for the first time in eight years became a real part of their lives. For me, Step Eight was a lesson in patience, faith in the program, and in God, and finally, a miraculous turning point in my program and in the life of my family.

---

[17] *Alcoholics Anonymous*, p. 83.

PRACTICING
THESE
PRINCIPLES

୧୬

Some of us could not understand what good could come from thinking about how we had hurt others in the past. Some had trouble focusing on how we had harmed others since the harm done to us seemed so great. To those of us for whom saying "I'm sorry" had become an unhealthy way of life, this Step seemed like a step backward rather than forward. Yet Step Eight is not about judging others or ourselves. It is an action Step that plays a critical role in developing the discipline of rigorous self-honesty. In Step Eight we expand the healing process begun in Step Four by naming those we had harmed. As we review the ways in which we have harmed others, the consequences of our actions become real and concrete.

In considering the Eighth Step, it is important to remember that, until we can take this Step in a spirit of self-love and healing, we may not be ready for it. Step Eight, like the other Steps, is a step toward healing. It is not about humiliating ourselves or making others feel better at our expense. It is about owning up to what we have done and becoming willing to free ourselves from the guilt and shame our actions have caused us.[18]

---

[18] *How Al-Anon Works for Families & Friends of Alcoholics*, p. 59.

As we begin, we ask our Higher Power for the honesty and willingness to do the work at hand, for the guidance we need and especially for help in bringing to mind those things we would rather forget. At first, we set aside how we will make the amends. We also set aside wrongs done to us and work on extending the same forgiveness to others that we ourselves will seek in Step Nine. We begin by noting how the defects uncovered in Step Four affected others and ourselves. Then, as thoroughly as possible, we list every relationship that needs healing, examining what we did, why we did it and the consequences of our actions. A sponsor or another program member can guide us, helping us to clarify where we caused harm and where we did not. Finally, we bring the list to our Higher Power and ask for the willingness to make amends as God directs and empowers us. Some of us have had to pray repeatedly and wait patiently for that willingness, but persistence here leads to success.

In Step Eight we take responsibility for our past actions, beginning the process of repairing the damage caused through our reactions to sexaholism or through the course of living an imperfect human life. This Step is simply about beginning to clean our side of the street, identifying the problems in our relationships that stand in the way of our continued spiritual development. It is often painful to survey "the wreckage of our past," but listing those we have harmed begins to release some of the guilt that has plagued us. Admitting how we contributed to past problems sets the healing process in motion, and we begin to feel more comfortable with ourselves and lose our fear of others.

One benefit of completing Step Eight is a growing conviction that the mistakes of the past can teach valuable lessons, helping us learn to accept the strengths and weaknesses in ourselves and others. We see that each relationship is a necessary part of our growth and learning. We begin to understand the words in *Alcoholics Anonymous*, "We will not regret the past nor wish to shut the door on it."[19]

---

[19] *Alcoholics Anonymous*, p. 83.

• • •

STEP EIGHT

*Made a list of all persons we had harmed, and became
willing to make amends to them all.*

✧ Have I put off making a list of persons I have harmed?
If so, why?

✧ Do I realize that forgiveness can begin with me? Do I understand
that a choice not to take the time necessary to work through feelings and forgive can be a choice to reject freedom and remain a
victim?

✧ Who was harmed by my behavior? To begin, I can review my
actions driven by the character defects as listed in my Fourth
Step inventory. Those harmed might include those close to me
such as members of my family, my spouse (or ex-spouse), my
children, my in-laws, my employer, and my friends. What about
myself? My Higher Power? People who have since died? People
who bore the brunt of my misdirected anger at the sexaholic,
perhaps the clerk in the store, the police or others?

✧ Who or what brings up my guilty or defensive feelings? Am I
reluctant to add someone to my list because "they did more
harm to me than I did to them?" In which relationships would I
like to have peace (even if I cannot or do not want to maintain
the relationship)? What are some program tools I can use to let
go of my reluctance?

✧ Have I included on my list anyone I falsely accused of causing
my pain or the sexaholic's problem? Those I tried to control or
manipulate? Those who were affected by my rage? Those I lied
to, blamed or shamed? Those about whom I gossiped? Those

with whom I broke commitments to be available for the sexaholic?

∞ What was the specific harm done in each case? Why did I do it? What are my thoughts and feelings about it? What were the consequences?

∞ Do I believe I need to put everyone I have ever come into contact with on my list? What is an appropriate balance?

∞ Have I asked my sponsor or other S-Anons about their list-making? What can I learn from them?

∞ How are willingness and humility related? Am I now willing to make amends? If not, what is holding me back? How can I become willing? How can God help me with this?

STEP NINE

*Made direct amends
to such people wherever possible,
except when to do so
would injure them
or others.*

We now take the list we made in Step Eight and make direct amends to those people we had harmed. We are ready to take responsibility for our past and the hurt we have caused others. We need discernment, good timing and courage to take this Step, but with God's help and guidance we will know whom to go to and when to make such amends. Each person will require a different approach. We need to know how much to disclose to each person, lest we do more harm than good. It is not always necessary to go into grim detail to make our amends.

We are actively repenting, which means "turning around" from our old ways toward new, considerate attitudes and actions. We need not wallow in excessive guilt or over-responsibility. Those feelings do not promote constructive action. We need to be honest and sincere, that is all.

As we look over the list of family, friends, and business acquaintances we have hurt, we may feel uneasy about discussing with them our spiritual principles or our involvement in S-Anon. We can rest assured this is not necessary. We are trying to put our own lives together and be of maximum use to God and others. People are more likely to be impressed with our sincere desire to set our wrongs right than with our programs or spiritual discoveries.

We have found it much harder to go to an enemy than a friend. It may be that such a person has done us more harm than we have done him or her. It is very difficult to lay our faults before someone who we fear will not receive us well. Nevertheless, we go in a forgiving spirit and admit our ill feeling with humility. We never criticize such a person or tell him or her what to do. We stick to our own faults in a calm manner. The outcome may be positive; the other person may even admit his or her fault. Yet it doesn't matter if we are not warmly received. We have taken the responsibility to do our part and in that we receive our satisfaction and spiritual growth.

When could it be harmful to make direct amends? It might be harmful if a third party is involved. Telling a spouse or a boss something that would disclose another person's faults or misdeeds may compound problems. There may be justifiable exceptions to this guideline, but we want to be cautious when we involve someone else. There is no rule of any sort; we merely suggest caution with some disclosures. It is important that our own conscience and our Higher Power be our guides here. We must take the time to plan conscientiously and to determine what is appropriate. It is often wise to discuss our plans with our sponsor or a spiritual advisor before going ahead with the amends.

Some wrongs can never be fully made right. But if we have the right heart we needn't worry. In some cases we cannot see people directly, so we send a letter. We try not to delay, for there is a long period of rebuilding ahead. We must be initiators. People need more from us than a simple "I'm sorry." We also need to change our behavior and attitudes.

One way we can do this is to open up to people if we have been isolating ourselves. Feeling vulnerable in this way can be frightening, but we can be assured of the support of our Higher Power as we choose the correct behavior and change in ways that make us healthier. We may want to try to increase our acceptance of the people around us, whatever stage of growth they are in. True amends is true change. To quote from the AA "Big Book": "The spiritual life is not a theory. We have to live it." [20]

---

[20] *Alcoholics Anonymous*, p. 83.

• • •

As I became willing and able to make amends to my children, God gave me opportunities to do so. I have shared some information about the S-Anon program with a daughter who lives nearby. She knows that her father and I attend program meetings weekly. One day, this daughter, her baby son and I went shopping together. In the course of our conversation she shared that she had been disappointed by my attitude and behavior at her wedding five years previously. "You were not there for me when I got married." I knew it was true. At that very time, her father was spiraling down into the depths of his sexaholism, and I was heading for my "bottom," too. I was so focused on my husband's problem that I could not muster the energy to be excited for my daughter. She went on to say that this had been the biggest day of her life, and I just did not seem to care. Fortunately, I had made enough progress in my recovery that I was able to hear this without offering explanations or excuses. I understood that part of my amends to her was listening uncritically to her feelings and acknowledging the truth that I had not been emotionally present for her then.

After sharing her hurt and disappointment, she went on to say how much she appreciates my interest in her child. Her father and I had spent the day in the hospital with them when the baby was born. When he was two months old, I took care of him for a few days while they painted their new home. She told me I am a terrific grandmother and that she could see that attending S-Anon meetings has changed me. She sees a new, softer-hearted, loving woman with whom she trusts her child. The Ninth Step has allowed this daughter and me to grow closer.

The Ninth Step is also providing a way back from the estrangement I had with my youngest daughter. In her hurt and anger over my leaving our home after learning of my husband's affairs, she cut off communication with her father and me. She moved into an apartment after graduating from high school and did not speak to us for two years, except when it could not be avoided. For some time, we did not know where she lived or what her telephone number was. After my spouse and I got back together, she increased contact with us slightly.

One day, I heard from another family member that this daughter had found work in a distant city. She was moving the very same weekend her brother and his family were also making a move. My spouse and I had an interesting dilemma: who should help whom? We decided that he would travel to assist the son, and I would help my daughter if she wanted my help. I contacted her and she was surprised by my offer. She agreed to let me help pack. As it turned out, I was the only one who was available to help her move that day. With tears and sniffles, she hugged me and thanked me for the assistance.

Making amends by reaching out and just being available for whatever relationship she wanted helped clean my side of the street. It also gave me another gift: our relationship has been improving ever since. Recently we spent an hour on the phone. She asked some in-depth questions about the disease of sexaholism and the recovery programs her father and I work. I am so grateful for the way this Step helped to restore my relationships with my children!

• • •

When I came to S-Anon, I felt that I had been wronged. In my hurt and damaged pride, all I could think of when I first heard Step Nine was how much I looked forward to the day when my recovering spouse would have to say "I'm sorry" for how he wounded me through his sexaholism.

As I began to work the program, I learned that my spouse was not the only one in our relationship who needed to say "I'm sorry." As my denial wore off, particularly through working Step One and Step Four, countless examples came to my mind of how I had hurt my husband, especially through ignoring, enabling, caretaking and rage.

When I got to Step Nine several years later, my amends to the sexaholic needed to be made on several different levels. First, I humbly told him how sorry I was for hurting him in the past, especially for the way my denial and minimizing had helped to keep his addiction going. I particularly apologized for not believing him — and angrily disagreeing with him — when he shared that he suspected he had a problem with compulsive sex.

Next, I made "living" amends through a changed attitude toward him and by diligently applying the Steps to my part in our relationship and the Traditions to our relationship as a whole. I actively put into practice the slogan "Let it begin with me."

Finally, I continue to make amends by sharing my story at open S-Anon meetings when asked. As I grow in self-honesty over time, I gain a new perspective on my past actions. When my husband hears the latest rendition of my story at these open meetings, he inevitably will say to me afterward that he did not know this piece or that piece. He says he is grateful for the new knowledge because it helps him better understand me and our past. It also gives him an appreciation for how far we have come. Step Nine certainly has helped heal wounds for both my husband and me, and it has freed us to have the trusting and genuine relationship we always wanted.

•   •   •

During our early adult years, my brother and I had a very strained relationship. I felt he had physically and emotionally abused me as a child. For my safety, I chose to become very remote from him. As time went by, what had once seemed like a necessary attitude of detachment became a punishing coldness. Working the Steps made it clear that my serenity depended on keeping my behavior "clean," regardless of the behavior of others. I knew it was time to make amends for my own punishing, abusive behavior, yet I felt stuck. I was afraid that if I made direct amends to my brother, he would attack me verbally. I needed to be able to make the amends safely.

I brought the problem of making this amends to my sponsor. She suggested I make a "living" amends. As a start, she suggested that each time I encountered my brother on the telephone or in person, I actively initiate a friendly "Hello, how are you?" — each and every time. After several months, I noticed that I was less tense around him. We actually seemed to be somewhat friendly with each other. This was certainly progress.

Her next suggestion was that whenever I was in his presence I should try to stay in the same room he was in, at least for a brief time. I had spent years going from room to room to avoid his presence at family gatherings. Staying put was very awkward for me initially, but as time passed, it became more comfortable. Slowly I began to have more compassion for him and began to separate my brother, the human being, from the sexaholism that affected all of us.

Over time we began to interact with one another. Today, I can ask his advice on topics about which he is knowledgeable. Our relationship has grown tremendously, and I am grateful because now we must all contribute and communicate to cope with our mother's Alzheimer's Disease. Does this improved relationship mean I have forgotten my brother's abusive behavior? No, but I have worked hard at my own healing in therapy and through Step work. I thank God for my recovery from the abuse and for the benefits I have received from following my sponsor's suggestions on this amends.

•   •   •

I first came to S-Anon years ago when my wife admitted her sexaholism, and I admitted my own need for help. When Steps Eight and Nine were discussed in meetings and I heard about placing my own name on the amends list, I honestly thought it was a stupid idea. Yet as I worked the program and began experiencing its gifts, the idea didn't seem quite so foolish anymore.

About a year ago, I started making an amends to myself by taking up the sport of golf. I had always wanted to play but never felt I had the time, having placed work and others ahead of caring for myself. The result was a great deal of resentment at others who "took up so much of my time," to say nothing of the lack of fun and relaxation in my life. So at age 55 I finally let go of that resentment and made the time to do something nice for me — just for me. It wasn't about making a living for my family or creating the right environment for my wife and kids or trying to impress people at work. It was just for me, and that really feels good. So now when I come into my office wearing my chartreuse pants and golf shirt in the morning, and my staff starts poking fun because they know I'm going to leave early and play golf that afternoon, I just smile.

•   •   •

PRACTICING
THESE
PRINCIPLES

✑

U nderstandably, most of us were hesitant, if not terrified, to make amends. We were afraid of becoming vulnerable and admitting our mistakes, and we were afraid of others' reactions. We remembered, though, that willingness is the key to our recovery and, with our Higher Power's help, set aside our fear. With a sincere desire to set our wrongs right, we prayed for guidance and began to tackle our Eighth Step list, setting a goal where possible for completing each amends.

In making amends, we do not grovel or wallow in excessive guilt, nor do we incessantly express regret or apologize for the actions of others. We clearly and sincerely apologize for how we have harmed others and offer to right the wrong if that is possible. Most of us found that brief, to-the-

> *With this Step, we have an opportunity to choose the kind of person we would like to become and the kinds of relationships in which we would like to be involved. By making amends, we admit that we are human like everyone else and cease to set ourselves apart from others.*[21]

---

[21] *How Al-Anon Works for Families & Friends of Alcoholics,* p. 60.

point admissions were better than long detailed explanations of the spiritual program we now work and what really went on back then. Being brief helps us guard against rationalization, justification, defensiveness and blame. We take care not to criticize or argue, even if the other person reacts angrily. Our task is simply to sweep our side of the street and do what we can to set our wrongs right.

Many have found it imperative to ask a sponsor or program member for help with this Step. They can guide us, helping us to see when direct amends might harm others, and offer ideas we may not have considered on the means and timing of amends. For example, they can help us determine the ways in which angry feelings (which are acceptable and for which amends are not necessary) may have been expressed inappropriately and harmed others (for which amends are necessary). A sponsor and other program members can help ensure that we do not relieve our guilt at the expense of others or place ourselves in danger.

We found it important to follow through and complete Step Nine, not just stop with the successes of our first amends. Step Nine is a test of personal honesty — only we will know whether we have made our amends. It is only through thoroughly completing this Step that we truly are set free and given peace of mind. We no longer have to deny our mistakes. Long-held guilt is released, and we take another giant step toward accepting ourselves as we are. With God's guidance we finally see a way to create the harmony we wanted between ourselves and others. The principles of admission, forgiveness, restitution and changed behavior that underlie Steps Four through Nine become a treasured, on-going way of living our lives.

•   •   •

STEP NINE

Made direct amends to such people wherever
possible, except when to do so would
injure them or others.

❧ As I review my Step Eight list, which direct amends do I need to make as soon as possible? Which amends have the potential for harming others, including third parties? Which amends should be deferred for now? Which amends should perhaps begin as "living" amends before being done verbally? Which amends need to be made in a non-direct way (for example, to those who have died, to those whose whereabouts are unknown, etc.)? Which amends am I most reluctant to make?

❧ Have I reviewed my Step Nine plans with my Higher Power and a sponsor or other person who understands my spiritual program? Have I planned what I want to communicate in my direct amends?

❧ In the cases where directly apologizing would harm others, how can I still make amends? Similarly, how can I make restitution to those who are no longer here? (Some ideas: writing letters that are not meant to be sent and reading them to a sponsor; praying for the other person; making a living amends by changed attitudes towards the other person; volunteering to help others in similar circumstances; donating to a charity, etc. God and a sponsor can provide insight on appropriate amends.)

❧ What are specific ways I can make amends to myself? How can I make amends to my Higher Power?

❧ With each person on my Eighth Step list have I: (1) admitted to God, myself, and another person where I was wrong, (2) apologized to the injured party wherever possible, stating specifically what I did, (3) made restitution where possible, and (4) changed my behavior so as not to repeat mistakes of the past? Are there any amends I have not made yet? What is holding me back?

❧ If I have completed Step Nine previously, do I currently have any relationships about which I have guilty or unresolved feelings? Is there anything on "my side of the street" that I need to clean up? If so, how and when can I work the principles of Step Nine?

STEP TEN

⚓

Continued to take personal inventory and when we were wrong promptly admitted it.

S tep Ten suggests that we continue to take personal inventory and make amends promptly for any hurtful behavior caused by our defects of character. We put our S-Anon way of life into practice every day, whether those days are easy or hard. We continue to look at our strong and weak points, and we let our Higher Power reveal our growth. We are able to admit and accept what we find and correct what is wrong.

This process does not take place overnight. It lasts a lifetime. When we clearly see our defects, we once again ask God to remove them. We tell someone else of our shortcomings and make amends if necessary. Love and patience are our operating principles. We are, for the most part, reacting sanely and calmly to others. Miracles are happening. We are not over-confident in our own power, but neither are we afraid. Every day we carry with us the desire to do God's will, not our own. This is how we stay in good spiritual and emotional condition.

In the past we rationalized our resentments and allowed them to become the motivation for our actions. We did not know how to distinguish between irrational rage and valid anger. We can easily fall back into our disease if we are not cautious here. Most of us have experienced the "emotional hangover" — the distressed feeling that is the direct result of yesterday's negative, emotional turmoil. When this happens, we swear we'll never do it again. When it does happen again, we usually find it is triggered by an over-involvement in one of our problems. We obsess, we go into a rage and the rage erupts inside of us, often affecting others. We take the same risks with other tempting disturbances like jealousy, envy, self-pity and hurt pride.

We certainly want to eliminate these episodes. If we do have "slips" and revert to our old behaviors, we know better how to regain our sanity, and it takes less time than it used to. We have found the best thing to do is to admit we are having difficulty and correct our behavior as soon as possible. At these times a spot-check inventory can be of great help in bringing us peace and sanity. This enables us to resolve our conflicts, leave them behind and to have more serenity. It keeps our spiritual house, our insides, clean.

We can do a spot-check inventory by admitting to God the exact nature of our wrongs, then calling an S-Anon member to share them. We may also want to write out our feelings, sharing them with a sponsor or group member as soon as possible. This keeps us from raging or pouting at the sexaholic or others and prepares us to communicate our feelings and needs more constructively. If we do find ourselves blaming, lecturing or trying to convince, we can work this Step the same way. We admit our mistakes to God, talk to an S-Anon member and then offer our amends if need be. We have learned not to carry around excess baggage for long. When we are wrong we admit it as soon as possible.

When we look at ourselves and others objectively, we see that all people, including ourselves, are to some degree spiritually and emotionally ill and frequently wrong. We have learned to accept this fact and practice patience and tolerance for ourselves and others. We see that we were unable to communicate our deepest longings and frustrations when we raged about them. We also see how self-defeating it is to continue to be hurt by people who, just like us, are trying to grow, even if their efforts are not obvious to us. This realization has helped us to stop making unreasonable demands and placing unrealistic expectations on those we love. To do so is only to be let down.

We have come a long way. Even when we try hard and fail, we can be glad, knowing that the pain of failure is transformed into experience, strength, and hope with each attempt at growth. Pain is the touchstone of all spiritual progress. Along the way we receive strength and inspiration from the God of our understanding, who has all knowledge and power. If we have surrendered our lives to His care, we have begun to sense that strength in us. We have become conscious of God's presence in our lives.

• • •

R ecently some S-Anon friends and I were reminiscing about our early days in the program. One friend good-naturedly shared how confusing it had been to listen to my sharing in meetings those first few years. I

Step Ten
STORIES

had no idea what she was talking about, so I asked her to tell me more. She said it seemed that I spoke in riddles and talked around things, as if I were hiding something. After thinking for a moment, I said, "Yes, that may be true."

That evening while doing my Tenth Step inventory, I reflected on what my friend had said, asking God to help me to be honest about my past and to grant me the openness to receive any new spiritual insight. I thought back to what I was like years ago and what brought me to S-Anon. I had been married to a sexaholic who was a well-known minister in the community. He feared his sexaholism would be discovered and he would lose his job. I took on that fear and believed it was my responsibility to protect him. Even after coming to S-Anon, I spoke in extremely veiled terms to avoid the possibility of anyone discovering who my husband was. My spouse ultimately rejected recovery, and we eventually divorced due to the effects of his sexaholism on our relationship, finances, children and his job security. I continued my S-Anon recovery, yet still found myself trying to "cover for him" in public.

Some of my actions probably were based in the reality that discovery of his addiction would have threatened his job. Upon further reflection as I inventoried, it occurred to me that I had "protected" him in order to protect myself — from shame. I had feared if my husband's sexaholism were made public, I would be labeled as a failure, failing as a wife to keep him happy and sexually satisfied. As I thought about it, I realized that this "failure" theme was a recurring one for me. Since childhood I had believed that I was not as good as others, that I was somehow undeserving and inadequate. My parents and others had made fun of my body's shape and size. They told me that they wished I was more like their friends' children, dressed me in clothes that did not fit and shamed me for being shy.

As I finished that evening's Tenth Step, I saw at greater depth how my fear of failure and inadequacy and the resulting character defects of control and over-responsibility had negatively influenced my life from childhood through adulthood. I thanked God for the gift of the S-Anon program and for giving me release one day at a time from fear, control and over-responsibility. My life is so very different now. As I work the program, personal shortcomings continue to be lifted at even deeper levels, and I am able to love and accept myself as I am and as I was created to be.

•　　•　　•

I was out of town on a business trip that involved more than the usual number of flight delays and rental car mix-ups. I checked into my hotel room well after midnight and decided to listen to my home telephone messages before going to bed. One of the messages let me know that I had broken the anonymity of some S-Anon members while doing program service work. Even though my error had been unintentional, the impact on others was real. I felt terrible! I immediately turned to my Higher Power for comfort and guidance.

It was obvious to me that I needed to work the Tenth Step and that I owed amends to each of the affected parties. I wanted to act right then to end the pain and discomfort I was feeling, but I could not call those I had harmed because of the late hour. I realize now that if I had made quick amends, I might easily have skipped the rest of Step Ten, depriving myself of its full benefits. To prevent similar painful situations, I needed to take a full inventory of my thoughts, actions and motives leading to this mistake. The forced delay in making amends was actually a gift from my Higher Power that allowed me to learn some valuable lessons.

As I reflected on the situation, it was clear how and why the error occurred. I had been very busy in every part of my life: school, job, home and program. I realized that I had allowed myself to become too busy and overwhelmed. In my worry that important things might be left undone, I had hurried through tasks that needed to be done at a thoughtful pace. I had lost sight of my initial purpose — to be useful to God and others. The result was a breach of one of the most fundamental principles of the program: anonymity. I was glad that I could make the amends phone calls when I returned home.

I am continually amazed by how cunning my old thinking and behavior are and how quickly my life can become unmanageable if I am not consciously working my program. I am very grateful that the Tenth Step and my Higher Power give me the tools to deal with and learn from painful situations as they arise.

•   •   •

On a particularly busy day at my job, I was rushing to get a newsletter ready for mailing before a meeting when I received a telephone call from the postal service. The woman on the line identified herself as a supervisor and in a kind voice began with the words, "I'm afraid I'm the bearer of some bad news." She explained that post office officials had determined that my employer's non-profit newsletter had violated a certain mailing requirement and

that we were not paying enough postage. She said they would col-
lect back payment of several thousand dollars for the last two years
— money our organization did not have. My fear of not being able
to pay turned immediately into defensiveness and then just as
quickly into anger and indignation — a pattern of character defects
I had developed in part through living with the disease of sexaholism. The supervisor became the unfortunate recipient of my self-
righteous indignation. I made accusations and gave full vent to my
anger. I ended the phone call and sat there at my desk, flooded with
feelings and obsessively reliving the phone call.

As the afternoon wore on, the angry feelings died down and I
noticed a tightness in my stomach and some emerging guilty feelings about how I had handled the phone call. I used a spot-check
inventory to examine the situation and determine what had
prompted my behavior. I acknowledged that the timing of the
phone call was unfortunate. Rushed as I was, that phone call did not
fit in with "my plans" for the day. My Fourth Step inventory had
shown me just how much I liked things in my control, and clearly
that defect had triggered part of my angry response. Thinking about
the call further, I saw that even though I disagreed with the post
office's interpretation of the situation, there was no reason to
explode at their employee. She was simply doing her job. It was
ironic how my old people-pleasing behavior had been transformed
with my recovery. Now I had no problem letting people know how
I felt, but this incident raised the question, "At what cost?" I pictured someone being as angry with me as I had been with that
supervisor, and that picture was not pretty. I knew my Higher
Power was teaching me to maintain a balance between stuffing feelings and voicing feelings appropriately.

I realized I needed to right this wrong, so I said a prayer asking
for God's help with what I was about to do, and I called the woman
back. She, of course, remembered me. I apologized for my actions,
briefly stating that while I disagreed with their interpretation of the
situation, that was no reason to be disagreeable. I asked her forgiveness for my rudeness, which she granted, saying that she really
appreciated my willingness to call back and apologize. I got off the
phone feeling clean, a burden lifted. I am so grateful that the Steps

of S-Anon do not only apply to overcoming the direct effects of living with sexaholism. They are also a formula for living every part of my life freely.

PRACTICING
THESE
PRINCIPLES

֎

In Steps One through Three we built a spiritual foundation. In Steps Four through Nine we took an inventory of past deeds and did what we could to right our wrongs. Once we have a clean slate, we maintain our clear conscience through the applications of Steps Ten, Eleven and Twelve.

Step Ten continues the recovery process of admission of our wrongs, forgiveness, and restitution that underlie Steps Four through Nine. Instead of compulsively focusing on others, we now commit to deliberate self-examination for the purpose of keeping close to God and our fellows and staying on course. This self-focus is not an obsessive drive for perfection or a perpetual dwelling

Learning daily to spot, admit, and correct these flaws is the essence of character-building and good living. An honest regret for harms done, a genuine gratitude for blessings received, and a willingness to try for better things tomorrow will be the permanent assets we shall seek.[22]

in the past, but rather a basic commitment to honesty and growth. In Step Ten we regularly take stock of our liabilities, looking particularly for selfishness, dishonesty, resentment and fear, as well as for

---

[22] [Alcoholics Anonymous] *Twelve Steps and Twelve Traditions*, p. 95

our progress, good choices, successes and gifts for which we can be grateful. We inventory honestly and avoid rationalizing and excessive guilt. We are compassionate with ourselves, acknowledging our own humanity. Step Ten helps us live in the real world, not in denial or fantasy. It gives us permission to admit our mistakes to ourselves and others and to take responsibility for any harm caused by our mistakes.

At its heart, Step Ten is a process of noticing the motives behind our thoughts, words, and actions. Our physical state can also give us information. Is the tenseness in our neck perhaps a sign of some anger we are not acknowledging? Is the tight feeling in our stomach possibly a result of shame over slipping into some old behavior that we had hoped to avoid? Is the lightness in our step related to the accomplishment of finally setting a long-needed boundary? Trusting that our Higher Power is guiding us, we make observations and reflections such as these, looking deeply for the real causes and motivations for our actions. If we see that we have harmed ourselves or others, we promptly make amends. If we discover a character defect, we can ask God to remove it. Through Step Ten we observe the daily nitty-gritty of our lives, making on-going, mid-course corrections and letting our lapses be lessons for growth. Done regularly, Step Ten keeps us in balance, free from unnecessary burdens and helps "make our lives more serene and fulfilling."

While we can make a regular, daily inventory in the morning or evening, other types of inventory are also helpful. Talking with a sponsor can help us admit the need for making amends to others or ourselves. "Spot-check" inventories done in the heat of emotional disturbance can help to clarify our part in the problem and any needed corrective actions. Periodic inventories at the end of a week, month or year reveal our growth and areas for improvement. We find that regular use of Step Ten can make us aware of old behavior and destructive thoughts more quickly. It helps us cultivate the practice of kindness, love, patience, tolerance and understanding, and further develops our connection with the Higher Power of our understanding.

• • •

STEP TEN

*Continued to take personal inventory and when we were
wrong promptly admitted it.*

❧ Do I set aside regular time for a Step Ten review? If no, why not?
What specific actions can I take to make Step Ten a priority in
my life? What form of personal inventory works best for me?
How might the Serenity Prayer relate to Step Ten?

❧ Who are some trustworthy people with whom I can "promptly
admit my wrongs?"

❧ What is my body telling me today? Do I have discomfort about
any lack of action on my part or about any interaction with others? With the sexaholic? Co-workers? Children? Relatives?
Friends? The person on the street? What part did I play in these
interchanges? What were my motivations?

❧ "Reviewing my day, where was I resentful? selfish? dishonest?
afraid? self-seeking? inconsiderate? Where did other character
defects crop up? Do I owe an apology? Am I keeping to myself
anything that needs to be discussed with another person? Was I
kind and loving today? What am I grateful for today? What
could I have done better? Was I thinking of how I could be of use
to God and others or simply intent on living life based on my
own will? For what can I ask forgiveness from God or others?
What corrective measures should be taken?" [23]

---

[23] Adapted from *Alcoholics Anonymous*, p. 86.

❧ Has my inventory revealed character defects that I can ask God to remove from my life? What positive traits has my inventory revealed that are increasing or progressing in my life and for which I can be grateful?

❧ As I think about the coming day, how can I be of best use to my Higher Power and others? How can I put into action this concept: "Thy will, not mine be done?"

STEP ELEVEN

♋

Sought through prayer and meditation
to improve our conscious contact with God
as we understood Him, praying only
for knowledge of His will for us
and the power to carry that out.

In S-Anon we use two principal means of establishing conscious contact with God: prayer and meditation. When we first came to the program, many of us recoiled at the thought of bowing before God. Many had strong logic which we thought proved that there was no God whatsoever. Maybe we conceded that a Higher Power of some sort existed, but there certainly wasn't any evidence of a God who knew or cared about people. However, we did come into S-Anon at least willing to open our hearts to new possibilities. At first, some of us looked to the S-Anon group as our Higher Power. Then, in time, we were able to consider a Higher Power to whom we could pray and meditate. We did this through experimentation, and when we did get results, we knew that there was power in prayer. Alcoholics Anonymous put it this way, "It has been well said that 'almost the only scoffers at prayer are those who never tried it enough.'"[24]

Prayer is simply talking to God. It is personal communication much like conversation with a trusted friend. Prayer can also

---

[24] [Alcoholics Anonymous] *Twelve Steps and Twelve Traditions*, p. 97.

include making requests to God. We use caution in asking for specific results for specific problems, being careful not to ask God to do it our way. We find it helpful to add to each petition "if it be Thy will." Those who have followed through with Step Eleven have found knowledge, experience, and peace of mind praying not for what we wanted or felt we deserved (the shopping list to God), but for His will only. According to the "Big Book," "We are then in much less danger of excitement, fear, anger, worry, self-pity, or foolish decisions."[25]

Some things may look like they are obviously God's will, but there is also God's timing to consider. We can ask for the grace and the patience to seek God's will for just one day at a time. Circumstances will always change tomorrow. We can be comforted by the fact that even hardships in life have a way of working toward the good for those who honor God.

In order to stay in proper balance, we would like to offer another word of caution: people who try to run their lives by claiming explicit guidance from God might easily and unconsciously rationalize their answers when they are not "answers from God" at all. With the best of intentions, these people might misinterpret God's will and create much confusion by forcing upon others their idea of God's will. This means they are living with a certain amount of presumption and pride. S-Anon experience shows that it is better to pray for God's will to be done not only in our lives, but in the lives of others as well, while not claiming to know what that might be. For example, we may think that all those who we perceive to be addicted or codependent need to be in Twelve Step recovery. We may be right in theory, but wrong about God's timing for another person. In this case we do well to remember "Live and Let Live."

What about meditation? To meditate is to ponder or to imagine. It is a time for ourselves when we can be quiet with God and within self and be inspired toward new revelations. The objective of meditation is always to improve our conscious contact with God. We

---

[25] *Alcoholics Anonymous*, p. 88.

start out slowly, perhaps contemplating the meaning of every word or phrase of our devotional readings and the thoughts of our hearts. If letting the mind wander into spiritual things seems a bit silly, remember how many times we used our imagination to enter our patterns of obsessive thinking. We are now learning to use our imagination in a constructive way. We might dwell upon a favorite prayer or other inspirational reading material from our individual faith tradition. We could choose to let our thoughts rest upon a beautiful and scenic place in nature: the beach, the mountains, or the desert. When we behold, through nature, the immensity of a Power greater than ourselves, we can perceive a world that is held in existence by a Creator.

The combination of self-examination, meditation and prayer gives us a foundation for living. The regular practice of prayer and meditation rewards us with emotional balance, a sense of belonging and knowing that God watches lovingly over us. Even when we feel cut off from our Higher Power's help and direction (which we all experience sometimes), we should simply resume prayer as soon as we can, doing what we know to be good for us. Our situation then becomes less disturbing and we begin to feel safer in the world. As we gain small glimpses of God's reality, we know our path will continue to lead us to greater knowledge of His will.

•   •   •

Step Eleven
STORIES

One of my most difficult decisions was whether to stay in or get out of my relationship with the sexaholic. I got a lot of advice from well-intentioned friends who suggested that I end the relationship and get on with my life. That idea was appealing on the days I was angry about what had happened and when I was frightened about the future. I was acutely aware that if he relapsed, I faced the possibility of infection with life-threatening, sexually transmitted diseases. I didn't know if I could live with that risk.

While agonizing over the decision, I considered my options. I avoided dwelling on the wrongs, real or imagined, that had been done to me. I also refrained from focusing on negative things I feared might happen in the future, making a conscious effort to forgo thoughts of "what-if." I had enough *real* problems to cope with in each 24 hours.

The quickest way I found to displace my frightened, resentful and obsessive thinking was deliberately redirecting my thoughts toward a spiritual idea, program slogan or prayer. I found suggestions throughout our S-Anon Conference-Approved Literature and found particular help in the prayer of St. Francis:

> Lord, make me a channel of thy peace — that where there is hatred, I may bring love — that where there is wrong, I may bring the spirit of forgiveness — that where there is discord, I may bring harmony — that where there is error, I may bring truth — that where there is doubt, I may bring faith — that where there is despair, I may bring hope — that where there are shadows, I may bring light — that where there is sadness, I may bring joy. Lord, grant that I may seek rather to comfort than to be comforted — to understand, than to be understood — to love, than to be loved. For it is by self-forgetting that one finds. It is by forgiving that one is forgiven. It is by dying that one awakens to Eternal Life. Amen."[26]

---

[26] [Alcoholics Anonymous] *Twelve Steps and Twelve Traditions*, p. 99.

The morning and evening prayer suggestions found on pages 86-88 of *Alcoholics Anonymous* were particularly helpful, too. I also found that intentionally setting aside time to seek a meditative heart and soul connection with my Higher Power helped me better discern God's direction. Through using Step Eleven in this way I was able to make constructive changes and thoughtful decisions in solving my problems.

Through practicing these principles and using all the tools of the S-Anon program, I decided to stay in the relationship. That was many years ago, and happily, it turned out to be a good decision for me. Now when making decisions concerning any area of my life, I know that anxiety and frustration are signs that I am relying on my own power and my own plan. That leaves God out entirely. My sponsor points out that I am in much less danger of such pitfalls when I make the effort to establish daily conscious contact with God. That is why I make an effort to start and end my day with prayer, meditation and self-examination. I also try to remember to pause and seek my Higher Power's will whenever I feel upset and to express my gratitude to God when I feel His presence and action in my life.

•   •   •

The first time my husband was arrested for voyeurism I was frightened for myself and my family. I lied to the police and attempted to provide an alibi for him. I chose to lie because I did not have the courage to face my fears. I was afraid of what everyone would think if they knew I was married to a "Peeping Tom." I was afraid of financial problems if he were to go to jail and lose his business. I was afraid he would be angry with me.

The depth of shame I felt was immense. I constantly obsessed about him, his behavior, what he would do next and how hurt and angry I felt. I vigilantly sought more and more ways to protect my family from future catastrophe. I was angry, afraid and exhausted.

Then I discovered S-Anon. I came to meetings and learned about boundaries and detachment: how to love someone without losing myself. I learned how to live in God's grace and I opened myself to experiencing my Higher Power's guidance. I got a sponsor, began working the Steps, used the telephone, talked with program members, and most importantly, listened to my Higher Power through the wisdom of others. The Serenity Prayer and "acceptance paragraph" on page 417 (fourth edition) of *Alcoholics Anonymous* became my guides for living each day.

Later, my husband was arrested again. This time I drew on the strength of my S-Anon recovery and my response was much different. I spoke honestly with the police and did not bail him out. While I often was afraid, I trusted that consequences to our family for my choice not to enable him would be manageable for us if we asked God for help. I separated from my husband, a consequence of further arrests. While following through with my boundary on this was very uncomfortable, I felt my Higher Power's presence and remembered the other difficult times when God had carried me through. I relied on Step Eleven and did as much as I could to be open to receiving God's help. I prayed and listened avidly for the voice of my Higher Power speaking to me through my S-Anon support network. I asked for God's will to be made plain to me, and I followed that to the best of my ability. I prayed for the best possible outcome for all of us, and I did not dictate what I thought that should be. I meditated, visualizing and feeling God giving me strength. I also connected with my Higher Power through everyday things like singing, noticing nature while walking and being emotionally present while blowing bubbles with my young son. All of this helped me feel the embrace of God. The discomfort of following through with the boundary passed.

Today, even though some things are not resolved with my husband, I am clear that everything is as it should be and that all will be well. I know that when I consciously seek my Higher Power I am at peace and unashamed.

• • •

My faith was an important part of my life long before I came to the S-Anon program. It gave me strength and encouragement when I divorced and became a single parent, began to work full-time and tried to juggle a busy schedule with two toddlers. I leaned on my Higher Power because that was all I could do. Fortunately, that was enough; I did not need to do anything more for God's help. During this time I was gifted with the knowledge of things I needed to change about myself and the ability to do so. One awareness was that I had been in a number of relationships with sexaholics. This insight led me to S-Anon.

After about five years of working the S-Anon program, I began to experience a stagnation and a sense of unrest regarding my Higher Power. I felt that my difficulty was due to the fact that I could not "see" God. For me, it was like trying to relate to a cloud. One morning during my regular meditation in which I visualize coming into God's presence, it came to me that I had a *relationship* with God, so all I had to do was practice my part. It made sense that if I brought the same attitudes, actions, and behavior that S-Anon had helped me learn to apply in my other relationships into the relationship with my Higher Power, this relationship would be enriched as well.

I began to practice the qualities of a good relationship, such as honesty, devoting my time and open-mindedness. When I made a conscious connection with God in the morning or in the evening, I began to feel that I was spending time with my very best friend, and it was a sweet experience for me. An added bonus was the growing knowledge that God wanted an intimate relationship with me, too. More and more I felt that I was being drawn into a deep kinship with my Higher Power.

In all my relationships, whether with people or with my Higher Power, I experience varying degrees of success. However, when my day begins and ends with focusing on my most important relationship, the one with God, the other areas of my life are much saner. I still experience normal ups and downs as well as some major curves, particularly when it comes to discerning God's will for me versus my own. As I continue to work Step Eleven, my growing relationship with my Higher Power invites me to practice tolerance, love and acceptance of myself, just as I am learning to exercise those qualities with others on their journeys. As my Higher Power strengthens my serenity, I am enabled to meet life's challenges and encouraged to grow into the person God created me to be.

• • •

A discussion on the Eleventh Step in an S-Anon couples meeting led me to question exactly how I could improve my conscious contact with my Higher Power. Even after many years of attending S-Anon and finding freedom from many of the effects of sexaholism, I was aware that I tended to forget my Higher Power during the day when things were going well. I decided to use a favorite prayer, the Third Step Prayer (found on page 63 of *Alcoholics Anonymous*), whenever possible during the day to improve communication with my Higher Power. I wanted to use this prayer to increase my conscious contact with God and as a reminder to humbly give myself over to my Higher Power. I made the commitment to stay open to whatever my Higher Power might show me and to carry out God's will to the best of my ability.

I decided to use my commuting time to begin the process. I was usually an angry, aggressive person behind the wheel, a habit I still had from the crazy days of reacting to sexaholism. I knew from recent Tenth Step inventories that this was an area of my life that required major revision. The first change I made was choosing to stay in one lane instead of weaving and racing through traffic. When traffic stopped or slowed to a crawl, I began my prayer. Whenever I was stopped at a traffic light, I recited the prayer, repeating it over and over until it was time to move again.

Before the month was over I sensed a welcome change in my attitude in many areas of my life. I found serenity on the roadways — abstinence from "road rage." I was feeling better about myself and about my relationships. Then my employer made cuts in staff, and I was one of those who lost their job.

Like virtually anyone in that situation, I suffered great anger and distress for several days. When I shared my feelings at my S-Anon meeting, the group helped me come to accept those feelings and also helped me to see what a great opportunity this was for me. The group became the source of my awareness of my Higher Power acting in my life, even in that situation. They could see the advantages of my position and the unlimited opportunities open to me to make a positive change in my line of work. I became aware that moving on to work that I loved was another way in which I could do my Higher Power's will for me. This realization put to rest the fear that God's will for me must always be unpleasant or downright burdensome. My group and I celebrated the change, and the fellowship has continued to support me as I have moved into a new career.

•   •   •

PRACTICING
THESE
PRINCIPLES

❦

S tep Eleven suggests prayer and meditation as spiritual communication tools for the continuing development of our relationship with the God of our
understanding and with ourselves. Regular spiritual practice helps us improve our
conscious contact with our
Higher Power and opens us to
God's love and grace. Through
Step Eleven we let go of relying
on a strictly analytical approach to problem solving. We
learn to include our intuition
and the wisdom and direction
of our Higher Power.

There is a direct linkage among self-examination, meditation, and prayer. Taken separately, these practices can bring much relief and benefit. But when they are logically related and inter-woven, the result is an unshakable foundation for life.[27]

It is interesting that this
Step refers to prayer *and* meditation, not prayer *or* meditation. Prayer generally is
considered simply to be talking
to our Higher Power. Our experience suggests that prayer can take
many forms. For many it is a religious act which might include

---

[27] [Alcoholics Anonymous] *Twelve Steps and Twelve Traditions*, p. 98.

folding hands, bowing the head, or kneeling. Some simply and freely express their thoughts and feelings to God. Others pray in a structured way by using religious prayers. Some write letters to their Higher Power. Others use a constant open conversation with God as their prayer. Some pray out loud; some pray silently. Some even sing spiritual songs. Whatever the method, it is clear that prayer as suggested in Step Eleven is not about begging or demanding that God grant our request. Rather in Step Eleven we show our willingness to surrender our will to our Higher Power, humbly inviting God to guide our thoughts and actions in a way that accomplishes greater purposes.

Meditation is often thought of simply as getting quiet enough to hear what has been described as "the still, small voice of God." Meditation has been used across time in many cultures, so there are many examples of how to practice meditation. Many of us found it helpful to work with others to learn how to meditate. Some common methods of meditation include a dedicated period of time for focusing on breathing and emptying oneself of troublesome thoughts, repeating prayers or phrases, practicing a mindfulness about each action during our day, concentrating on a single idea or image, or constructively imagining ourselves placing our troubling situations in the care of our Higher Power. Even though many of us initially felt meditation would be a waste of time, it was not long before we found it to be an indispensable, energy-enhancing activity we could not go without, just like eating or breathing. Especially when combined with prayer and the self-examination of Step Ten, we found that meditation balanced us emotionally and provided a deeper connection with our Higher Power.

•   •   •

STEP ELEVEN

*Sought through prayer and meditation to improve our conscious contact with God **as we understood Him**, praying only for knowledge of His will for us and the power to carry that out.*

❧ What does "conscious contact with God" mean to me? What does "improving" it mean? How can I build on my spiritual strengths?

❧ What influences or role models have I had for prayer and meditation? Have these influences and role models made my relationship with God easier or more difficult? Do I have a fear of intimacy with my Higher Power or a concern that my prayer and meditation will not be "good enough?"

❧ What keeps me from practicing Step Eleven? How can I address any obstacles that may stand in my way?

❧ It is said that the only way to fail at prayer and meditation is to not make time for them. Am I too busy for God? Am I willing to make the development of a relationship with my Higher Power a priority in my life? How can I make room for prayer and meditation in the busyness of my life? Am I willing to explore various forms of prayer and meditation to find methods that suit me?

ℝ What does "praying only for knowledge of His will for us and the power to carry that out" mean? When I pray for other people, how can I keep to the spirit of "praying only for knowledge of His will for us?" What tools of the program can help me determine if the messages or inspirations I receive represent my Higher Power's will rather than my own self-will or rationalizations? How has God empowered me in the past?

ℝ Most people occasionally struggle with prayer and meditation. When I experience a spiritual dry spell, what can I do? How might the slogan "Act as if..." be helpful?

ℝ Looking back on my Step Two work and considering the ways I have experienced my Higher Power's presence in working Steps Three through Ten, are my ways of praying and meditating still appropriate today for contacting the God of my understanding? If not, what other forms of prayer and meditation might better suit my life today? Have I asked my Higher Power for help in this area?

STEP TWELVE

✺

Having had a spiritual awakening
as the result of these Steps,
we tried to carry this message
to others, and to practice these principles
in all our affairs.

What is a spiritual awakening in our S-Anon program? It is the ability to do, feel and believe, through God's power, that which a person could not do before with his or her own power. We have awakened to a concept of a loving God in our lives. This spiritual awakening is a gift that raises us to a higher level of awareness and gives us hope. We truly have been changed. We have received the grace of God, which simply means "a free gift." We find ourselves experiencing a degree of honesty, tolerance, unselfishness, serenity and love which seemed so hard to reach before recovery. We receive the precious gift of serenity by practicing the Twelve Steps.

Beginners who doubt themselves and their ability to progress can be viewed objectively by the rest of the group as we see the positive changes taking place in their lives. The person who claims that he or she does not understand the "spiritual angle" can predictably come to have conscious contact with God.

"Freely you have received, now freely give ..." is the motto of Step Twelve. Even the newcomer finds a rewarding experience in carrying the message to others who want the help of S-Anon. Although our own characters are still in need of much work, we have been greatly helped by encouraging others to find recovery, new purpose and meaning in life. We are seeing the lives of men and women who share our message change from darkness to light and from despair to hope. We can help others who are suffering from the effects of sexaholism better than anyone else can.

There are many ways to carry the message. The changes in our lives speak the loudest. We can be ready to answer anyone who may notice and inquire as to how those changes came about. Also, we bring our message to others each time we share in a meeting or stay after the meeting to talk to newcomers. We carry our message when we make telephone calls or perform service of any kind for the group.

> Carrying the message means personal one-to-one sharing with one another. It means giving moral support, standing by and listening, without criticizing or condemning, to the troubles and misfortunes of another person and helping him or her to find the path we have found. It means sharing love and experience with the unhappy newcomer who blames another for everything that went wrong, just as we used to do before our eyes were opened. It means being willing to help the long-time member who still finds it hard to apply the principles of the program to daily living.[28]

What about practicing these principles in all our affairs? Can we bring the same love and tolerance we are developing in the S-Anon group to our families, personal relationships, and work relationships? Yes, we can begin. This is how further spiritual development occurs. We have seen the importance of "walking the walk," not just "talking the talk."

We found that our old habit of following our impulses needed revision, because some of our impulses lead us into rage, fear and irrational thinking. We learned that giving in to those impulses was not always the best choice for our emotional serenity. As we placed our spiritual growth first, we discovered a better way of living for ourselves and those around us.

We surely have come a long way since the time when our desperate need for emotional security drove us into unworkable

---

[28] *Al-Anon's Twelve Steps and Twelve Traditions*, p. 76.

relationships. We had either dominated others or been overly dependent upon them. We had played games, putting ourselves in the position of the victim, the rescuer or the persecutor. At times we interchanged all of those roles. Some of us blamed others, not seeing our unreasonable demands. Now we see that too much dependence on people is unsuccessful because all of us are fallible. Even the best person might fail us, especially when our demands for attention are unreasonable.

We now find that the best source of emotional stability is our Higher Power, or God as we understand Him. S-Anon's Tradition Two suggests that we depend upon one authority, "a loving God as He may express Himself… " His perfect love and forgiveness turns all fear away. We found that freedom from fear was more important to us than adhering to impulsive habits from the past. It was quite revealing to find out how many of us were overly fearful.

Today we have gained confidence, trust, and knowledge of God. We see that our Higher Power requires us but to "do justice, love mercy and to walk humbly with our God." We have seen many miracles in our lives and are confident that the road ahead leads toward higher levels than we would ever have dreamed possible.

•   •   •

A popular discussion topic of many meetings I go to in S-Anon is "spiritual awakening." Over the years of my recovery, I have come to think of a spiritual awakening as "becoming aware of the obvi-
ous." My awakenings have always been so simple and right in front of me, but early on I would usually miss them because I was lost in my "how my relationship should be if only…" fantasy. Diligently working the Steps gradually removed the fantasy and revealed the obvious insights that were just waiting for me.

One of my earliest program awakenings was that I did not need to recount every second of my day for my husband. I am afraid that I had a habit of talking my husband to death! After my awakening about this behavior, I set a simple (and, as it turned out, very powerful) boundary for myself: I allowed him to ask about what he wanted to know. For awhile it was very quiet around our house, but keeping my boundary created an opportunity for him to start talking and now he participates in all our conversations.

I continued to go to my meetings each week and work the Steps. I found that "practicing these principles in all my affairs" became a natural process and resulted in even more awakenings. I started to look at every aspect of my life through the lens of the Steps. I looked at my children and made an inventory of what I could do to help them grow up secure and safe. This included modeling how to live honestly, teaching them to voice their feelings appropriately, and setting aside my fear in order to resolve my children's chronic medical issues. I looked at my work site and admitted that my over-responsibility there had made my life unmanageable. So I examined my own needs and determined what I could change, what I could not change and how much effort I could realistically put into my job. I looked at my relationship with my family of origin and set boundaries for myself, such as not taking others' inventories. Today I have a much more workable relationship with my family.

The S-Anon program has helped me learn to look for a lesson or spiritual awakening in all my experiences. My growth in recovery has come down to a simple formula for me: go to one or more meetings each week, study the Steps and Traditions with my sponsor and put them into practice, make phone calls and be of service to others through the Twelfth Step whenever I can.

• • •

During one weekend visit from my mother, I sat at my kitchen table just as the sun began to embrace the day. I had risen extra early to be able to read my meditation books before any one else got up, so naturally I felt a bit disappointed as I heard Mom come into the room to join me, pouring herself a cup of coffee. She asked what I was reading. After silently praying for acceptance before I responded, I looked at her and noticed a new softness and even an open yearning in her face. I felt a gentle inspiration from my Higher Power to read several paragraphs of the day's meditation aloud. After I finished reading, I shared my gratitude for the healing God had brought into our lives and relationship.

We had spoken before of the incest in our family and now with tears in her eyes, my Mom spoke again of her sorrow for not seeing sooner what Dad was doing, for not being stronger, for not being smarter. I looked into her weary eyes and told her that I finally knew she had no power to control Dad's disease. I told her I now realized that she had been just as much a victim of this family disease as my brother, sisters, and I had been, and that I also now understood how this disease had swallowed Dad, too. Remembering how each of us children had been sexually abused and how even the family dog had not been spared from the effects of this disease, I told my Mom that I also had struggled with feelings of guilt and shame because I had not been able to protect anyone.

As we cried together, I reached across the table to hold her hand. Our eyes connected, and it was as if time stood still, as images came to mind of the awakenings God had provided to me through working the Steps. I had become aware of why I had gotten into successive relationships with sexaholics. I had been willing to face painful flashbacks that seemed to swallow me whole at times, but ultimately helped me to face reality. I had been able to let go of blaming my mother for what my father had done and to let go of blaming myself, too. I had grieved the deep sadness from my childhood, layer by layer, as I healed and rose above it. I was filled with gratitude for my mother's courage to look at her part in the family disease, too, and her willingness to talk about it.

In that moment, I thanked God, who had made possible the healing found in S-Anon. I was grateful, too, for how my husband, who really wants to be set free from lust and has been willing to go to any length for recovery, has helped me find my own recovery from the pain and shame brought by the first sexaholic in my life — my father.

Mom has no S-Anon group, but I can still carry the message of experience, strength, and hope to her. What I have practiced for years in meetings is beginning to be practiced in "all my affairs" and all my relationships, even the ones that had been so shattered before. As devastating and shameful as the disease of sexaholism can be, it does not compare to the richness of the continual spiritual awakening, renewal and healing that God has brought into my life. I am astounded by God's ability to free so many of us by His message of truth, as He weaves our healing with that of those around us when we follow His lead and carry the message.

•   •   •

I did not come willingly to Twelfth Step work. My sponsor, the S-Anon literature and other meeting members suggested to me that while it is very important to work all Twelve Steps, I did not necessarily need to finish Steps One through Eleven before starting Step Twelve. In fact, it was suggested that doing Twelfth Step work (and focusing on something other than myself and my problems) would help me with the other Steps and with opening myself to receiving God's spiritual awakenings. Yet I was still reluctant to do such things as volunteer to lead a meeting, come early to set up or stay after to clean up. I realize now that this Twelfth Step action was hard because it confronted the nature of my problem: denial and isolation.

The members of my S-Anon group continued to gently say, "Take the action and the feelings will come." Slowly I began to do one bit of simple service — I stayed late to help clean up and began to talk with others. After a time, I volunteered to lead a meeting and found it helped me to be more honest with myself. I noticed that as I gave my time to the fellowship, I felt like less of an outsider and felt more accepted as a male in what I initially had labeled a "sorority."

Later, I was approached by another male member in S-Anon with the idea of starting a special semi-monthly men's S-Anon meeting to supplement our attendance at general S-Anon meetings. Again, my initial reaction was to stay isolated and let someone else do it, but instead I "took the action" and stopped worrying about it. We began to meet and soon realized that not only did we need to connect with other men, we needed to become involved in the larger S-Anon fellowship, too. In a group conscience, we agreed to send a representative from our special meeting to our local inter-group. Surprisingly, I found myself volunteering for that role.

Each time I ventured into Twelfth Step activity I would initially cringe, thinking, "How can I do this? What do I have to offer?" and, of course, "I don't have the time!" or "I don't want to!" Yet as I have worked the Steps, and especially the Twelfth Step, the clamor of fearful and self-doubting thoughts has steadily grown softer and shorter. I have seen my denial and isolation decrease, my confidence increase and spiritual awakenings from my Higher Power multiply. I have come to see the truth in the statement "As I give to the world, so the world will give to me."

•   •   •

I tried to cope with the sexaholism in our home in many ways — denial, rage and emotional withdrawal were only a few. However, the S-Anon approach is the only one that truly helped me recover from sexaholism's effects. Working the Steps of this program has given me a serenity and spiritual awakening I did not know were possible. That is why I do whatever I can to be a "trusted servant" when I carry the S-Anon message. For example, I speak up when S-Anon's Twelve Traditions are not followed in meetings, reminding those present of our group's commitment to the meeting sharing guidelines. Speaking up is not easy for me, but I know that to say nothing while a member or even the group itself by-passes the structure we have established to ensure unity is to passively participate in the decline of our group's ability to carry the message that each of us affected by sexaholism seeks.

The gratitude I have for this program also leads me to carry the message by making an extra effort to welcome newcomers and to help them understand the program. Whether it is answering the phone line, leading a newcomers' meeting or making a point to warmly greet newcomers before and after meetings, I try to remember that carrying the message is the primary purpose of our fellowship. Without the newcomer, S-Anon would eventually cease to exist. On a personal level, I know that the painful stories of the newcomer remind me of the importance of continuing to work the program in my own life.

Working my program also means that I carry the message through sponsorship and service work in general. Doing anything I can to contribute, no matter how small, helps to carry the message and enhance my recovery as long as I give freely without expectations or strings attached. I have learned so much through sponsoring others in this program: a deeper understanding of the Steps and Traditions, increased awareness of my own strengths and defects, a growing confidence that God will guide my sponsorship if I ask, etc. Carrying the message has strengthened my own recovery and helped me realize the gifts of the S-Anon program, especially my ability to give and receive love.

I am forever grateful that someone was there for me when I desperately needed the help and hope of S-Anon. That gratitude motivates me to continue to carry the message of my own recovery to other family members and friends of sexaholics who want the help of the S-Anon program.

•   •   •

PRACTICING
THESE
PRINCIPLES

W orking the Steps has given each of us spiritual awakenings, some dramatic and some so gradual they can only be seen through hindsight, yet our experiences have much in common. We can now do what we had previously been unable to do on our own. We have been transformed through accepting the help of a Higher Power, a previously underused source of strength. We have experienced the freedom of knowing that God's help is always within reach. We have reached a new level of honesty, inner peace and love. Working the Steps

> *We have found a new way of life...and to keep what we have found, we have to continue appreciating the gift and giving it away.* [29]

has given us conscious contact with God and a rebirth of our own spirit. Living the Steps has given us new purpose, and we find that we are much more able to accept each challenge we may face as an opportunity for further growth.

We see that in order to keep the spiritual life and serenity we now have, we must make a practice of "giving it away" through our words and actions. We carry the message of hope found in our own story: how our lives have changed as the result of working the Twelve Steps of S-Anon. No matter how we carry the message —

---

[29] *Paths to Recovery: Al-Anon's Steps, Traditions and Concepts*, p. 119.

through welcoming and working with newcomers, active listening and sharing in a meeting, sponsoring others, serving the fellowship or in the many other ways to work Step Twelve — we expect nothing in return beyond the promised "Gifts of the S-Anon Program." Rather, working Step Twelve is "gratitude in action" for what we have received. Our reward is the satisfaction of seeing lives changed. We know that our experience, though painful, has been transformed and can benefit others.

Practicing our program outside of S-Anon meetings can be difficult at times, but when we extend these spiritual principles into our daily lives, we enjoy a growing emotional maturity and become aware of even more spiritual awakenings. Using the principles of the Twelve Steps, we find that we can detach where we previously were obsessed. We develop compassion for those we had found unlovable. We respect ourselves. We are able to do what we never had been able to do before. We learn to assume our responsibilities and let others do the same. We know that whatever comes, our program and our Higher Power will help us to live fully and deal with problems as they arise. The gifts of the S-Anon program are truly ours.

•   •   •

STEP TWELVE

Having had a spiritual awakening as the result of these Steps, we tried to carry this message to others, and to practice these principles in all our affairs.

❦ What is the spiritual awakening I have had in working the Twelve Steps? Has it been a sudden awakening or a more gradual one? How has it changed my life?

❦ Have I worked all the Steps, allowing myself the full benefit of the spiritual awakening promised in Step Twelve? Are there Steps I have avoided? If so, why? What commitment can I make to working these Steps?

❦ What message do I carry? How have I tried to carry the message? Is my message focused on the Steps, Traditions and principles of this program or is it blurred with therapies and outside issues? How can I carry the message without giving advice or being intrusive?

❦ What types of Twelfth Step work do I do well? How has God worked through me in this Step? How can I pass on what I have learned regarding this particular Twelfth Step work?

❦ Are there types of Twelfth Step work I do not do? What is holding me back? What experiences might I be depriving myself of?

❦ How can Twelfth Step work help me find the right balance between over-responsibility and under-responsibility? What part can service in S-Anon play in my recovery? When I work with or sponsor others, how can I help them without taking on their problems? Do I carry the message rather than the person?

∞ What principles of the S-Anon program do I find easy to practice? Which ones do I find difficult to practice? How can I build on successes while expanding my use of the principles?

∞ How have I demonstrated the phrase "the changes in our lives speak the loudest?" What are specific ways that I can extend the qualities, attitudes and principles I have experienced in S-Anon meetings and "practice them in all my affairs?"

∞ The chapter on Step Twelve in the *Twelve Steps and Twelve Traditions* of Alcoholics Anonymous suggests that "practicing these principles in all our affairs" implies that we put our spiritual development ahead of our drives for emotional and financial security, personal prestige and power, romance and family satisfaction. That is, that "the satisfaction of these instincts cannot be the sole end and aim of our lives."[30] What priority does spiritual development have in my life?

---

[30] [Alcoholics Anonymous] *Twelve Steps and Twelve Traditions*, p. 114.